Grief's Wisdom:
Quotes that Validate the
Transformative Process

Compiled by:
John M. Schneider, Ph.D.

Cover photo "Skipping Stones" by Sharon Olson.

Grief's Wisdom:
Quotes that Validate the Transformative Process
ISBN: 0-9638984-5-0

Seasons Press, 526 W. 14th St., Suite 153
Traverse City, Michigan, 49684
www.seasonscenter.com

Acknowledgements
and Explanations

Collecting quotations on loss and grief began with my classes at Michigan State University on the psychology of loss and grief. Over the years, students and colleagues, clients and friends, learned of my interest, and shared their favorites. Often the quotes taught us humility— what we thought were new ideas, new ways of looking at grieving turned out to have been expressed long ago, and usually with more eloquence. We learned that grieving was not a new invention of the twentieth century, but something we shared with peoples of all times.

I am deeply appreciative of all of the contributions so many people have made to this anthology. Many more quotes were shared than appear here, not because they lack merit, but because I wanted to avoid sharing too much of a particular modern author's work or because I could not determine its reference source.

The citations for the quotations and poems in this collection follow the style utilized by *Bartlett's Familiar Quotations* in its Sixteenth Edition. That is to say, no underlining or quotation marks have been used. Instead, reference information is in italics following the author's name. A number of primary sources have been used as references, as have several works of quotations already in print, including *Bartlett's* in both its Sixteenth and Fourteenth editions and *Quotations By Women* by Rosalie Maggio. In choosing what information to include in our citations, we have made every effort to simplify and to be consistent while still retaining sufficient information so that you, the reader, may dig further on your own if you so desire.

I also wish to express my appreciation for Rebecca Chown and her attention to the details and the flow of this project. She's added a number of her own favorite quotes along the way. And many thanks to Dave Johnson for the marketing, design, and production support.

Most of all, I deeply appreciate the wisdom of all those authors whose works are quoted here. Each quote adds something to the whole—together they become all the more impressive as a collection of grief's wisdom across the ages.

Seasons
CENTER for Transformative Grief

Information • *Resources* • *Support* • *Tools*

**A new website for grief caregivers
and those in grief.**

www.seasonscenter.com

Website Features

Online bookstore

Articles and content on transformative grief

Life Change Self-test Inventory©

Grief-Depression assessment tools and content

Personal tales of transformation

Response to Loss Inventory©

Reviews of relevant books, music and films

Links to important resources and communities

Inspirational quotes—updated daily!

Sign-up for free monthly e-letter

This book is a companion volume to
Finding My Way:
Healing and Transformation Through Loss and Grief
(Seasons Press, 1994).
It is available online at www.seasonscenter.com

Contents

Section One *Discovering What's Lost*   1

Holding On   3

Letting Go   15

Becoming Aware   31

Section Two *Discovering What Remains*   53

Healing and Solitude   55

Gaining Perspective   67

Section Three *Discovering What's Possible*   83

Integration   85

Rethinking and Self-empowerment   121

Transformation   147

Discovering What's Lost:
The Ways We Cope
and Become Aware

I f we are to discover the light—
what we have left and what we can do with it—then discovery of
what we have lost must precede it. Awareness of grief is joy's
shadow. It measures the depth and breadth of our attachments.
During this time we comprehend that we will die someday. We
observe what is gone without the benefit of accomplishments or
the distraction of leading a meaningful life. Loneliness seems to
have no limit, no end.

We struggle against this cruel reality, fight it, and question
its fairness. Does anyone care? Can anyone know our grief?

The awareness phase of grief is:

+ A time of reckoning.
+ A time to accede to limits.
+ A time of emptiness.
+ A time to acknowledge how much of our life is over.
+ A time to mourn.
+ A time of sadness.

Awareness is the phase of grief that is central to mourning,
the most painful, lonely, helpless, and hopeless of times we will

ever face. Whereas we were not able to admit the depth of our loss previously—with our coping strategies of holding on and letting go—we are now entering a time of deepest pain and suffering. If there's a time when we choose to live or die, it's in the awareness phase.

The first question that must be addressed in grieving involves discovering the full extent of what has been lost—that is, finding out how extensive the loss is. This is the most difficult and most essential part of grief, for to discover what is left and what can be done with it, discovery of what has been lost must accompany the loss.

At first, most people attempt to cope with the overwhelming feelings of a loss in one of two ways. The first is called "holding on." When we "hold on," we fight to survive. We try harder to understand why our loss happened and to find a cure for it. We keep active, trying to create a distraction from our loss. We often take good care of others, yet we also expose our vulnerabilities in the hope that we will be able to regain, restore, or somehow win back what we have lost.

The other type of coping is commonly known as "letting go." When we "let go," we limit the amount of pain or stress we feel by *separating* from what was lost. We try to hide from our loss and to escape through our dreams and fantasies, as if in a trance or stupor. We limit our vulnerability by becoming passive or separated from everyday life, though we may engage in pastimes and socialize with friends to give ourselves a break.

For caregivers, it is important to realize that coping by reducing the awareness of a loss is normal and healthy—one should not try to push someone too fast toward "dealing with their loss." Both types of coping are normal, though people typically favor one over the other.

The quotes that follow in this section address the issue of what has been lost and the ways that people cope. Hopefully, reading about the grief others have faced will help you to deal with your own overwhelming loss.

Holding On

. . . . .

Pride goeth before destruction,
and an haughty spirit before a fall.

PROVERBS 16:18

. . . . .

I am holier than thou.

ISIAH 65:5

. . . . .

Nobody likes the man who brings bad news.

SOPHOCLES (C. 495-406 B.C.), *ANTIGONE*, L. 277

. . . . .

The fear of death is more to be dreaded than death itself.

PUBLILIUS SYRUS (1ST CENTURY B.C.), *MAXIM 511*

. . . . .

I have often regretted my speech, never my silence.

PUBLILIUS SYRUS (1ST CENTURY B.C.), *MAXIM 1070*

. . . . .

Absence makes the heart grow fonder.

SEXTUS PROPERTIUS (C. 54 B.C.–A.D. 2), *ELEGIES*, II, XXXIII, 43

. . . . .

To know that you do not know is the best.
To pretend to know when you do not know is a disease.

LAO-TZU (C. 604–C. 531 B.C.), *THE WAY OF LAO-TZU*, 67

. . . . .

Be not angry that you cannot make others as you wish them to
be, since you cannot make yourself as you wish to be.

THOMAS Á KEMPIS, *IMITATION OF CHRIST* (C. 1420), BK. I, CH. 16

. . . . .

. . . since love and fear can hardly exist together, if we must
choose between them, it is far safer to be feared than loved.

NICCOLÓ MACHIAVELLI, *THE PRINCE* (1532)

. . . . .

You may my glories and my state depose,
But not my griefs; still am I king of those.

WILLIAM SHAKESPEARE, *KING RICHARD THE SECOND* (1595), ACT IV, SC. I, L. 192

. . . . .

True is it that we have seen better days.

WILLIAM SHAKESPEARE, *AS YOU LIKE IT* (1599-1600), ACT. II, SC. VII, L. 120

. . . . .

Men prize the thing ungain'd more than it is.

WILLIAM SHAKESPEARE, *TROILUS AND CRESSIDA* (1601-1602), ACT I, SC. II, L. 313

. . . . .

God give them wisdom that have it; and those that are fools,
let them use their talents.

WILLIAM SHAKESPEARE, *TWELFTH-NIGHT* (1601-1602), ACT I, SC. V, L. 14

. . . . .

The weariest and most loathed worldly life
That age, ache, penury, and imprisonment
Can lay on nature, is a paradise
To what we fear of death.

WILLIAM SHAKESPEARE, *MEASURE FOR MEASURE* (1604), ACT III, SC. I, L. 127

. . . . .

Better to be quarreling than lonesome.

IRISH PROVERB

. . . . .

Hang there like fruit, my soul,
Till the tree die!

WILLIAM SHAKESPEARE, *CYMBELINE* (1609-1610), ACT V, SC. V, L. 264

. . . . .

I am two fools, I know,
For loving, and for saying so
In whining poetry.

JOHN DONNE (1572-1631), *THE TRIPLE FOOL*, ST. 1

. . . . .

The dignity of truth is lost with much protesting.

BEN JONSON, *CATILINE'S CONSPIRACY* (1611), ACT III, SC. II

. . . . .

O God! O God! that it were possible
To undo things done; to call back yesterday!
That Time could turn up his swift sandy glass,
To untell the days, and to redeem these hours.

THOMAS HEYWOOD, *A WOMAN KILLED WITH KINDNESS* (1607), SC. XIII

. . . . .

[The rich] are indeed rather possessed by their money than
possessors.

ROBERT BURTON, *THE ANATOMY OF MELANCHOLY* (1621-1651). DEMOCRITUS
TO THE READER, PT. I, SEC. 2, MEMBER 3, SUBSEC. 12

. . . . .

For "ignorance is the mother of devotion," as all the world
knows.

ROBERT BURTON, *THE ANATOMY OF MELANCHOLY* (1621-1651). DEMOCRITUS
TO THE READER, PT. III, SEC. 4, MEMBER 1, SUBSEC. 2

. . . . .

Let's meet, and either do or die.

JOHN FLETCHER, *THE ISLAND PRINCESS* (1647), ACT II, SC. II

. . . . .

Hell is full of good meanings and wishings.

GEORGE HERBERT, *JACULA PRUDENTUM* (1651), NO. 170

. . . . .

Living well is the best revenge.

GEORGE HERBERT, *JACULA PRUDENTUM* (1651), NO. 524

. . . . .

He hath no leisure who useth it not.

GEORGE HERBERT, *JACULA PRUDENTUM* (1651), NO. 897

. . . . .

Who overcomes
By force hath overcome but half his foe.

JOHN MILTON, *PARADISE LOST* (1667) BK. I, L. 648

. . . . .

We confess to little faults only to persuade
ourselves that we have no great ones.

FRANÇOIS, DUC DE LA ROCHEFOUCAULD, *REFLECTIONS; OR, SENTENCES AND
MORAL MAXIMS*, (1678), MAXIM 327

. . . . .

I have made this letter longer than usual, because I lack the
time to make it short.

BLAISE PASCAL, *LETTRES PROVINCIALES* (1656-1657), NO. 16

. . . . .

The greatest weakness of all weaknesses is to fear too much to
appear weak.

JACQUES BÉNIGNE BOSSUET (1627-1704), *POLITIQUE TIRÉE DE L'ECRITURE SAINTE*

. . . . .

Those who are believed to be most abject and humble are
usually most ambitious and envious.

BENEDICT (BARUCH) SPINOZA, *ETHICS* (1677), PT. III, PROPOSITION 29:
EXPLANATION

. . . . .

All is for the best in the best of all possible worlds.

VOLTAIRE (FRANÇOIS MARIE AROUET), *CANDIDE* (1759)

. . . . .

We must cultivate our garden.

VOLTAIRE (FRANÇOIS MARIE AROUET), *CANDIDE* (1759)

. . . . .

I quickly laugh at everything, for fear of having to cry.

PIERRE DE BEAUMARCHAIS, *LE BARBIER DE SÉVILLE* (1775), ACT I, SC. II

. . . . .

Misery still delights to trace
Its semblance in another's case.

WILLIAM COWPER, *THE CASTAWAY* (1799), L. 59

. . . . .

And while that face renews my filial grief
Fancy shall weave a charm for my relief
 Shall steep me in Elysian reverie,
A momentary dream, that thou art she.

WILLIAM COWPER (1731-1800), ON RECEIVING A PORTRAIT OF HIS MOTHER
WHO HAD DIED WHEN HE WAS SIX

. . . . .

No young man ever thinks he shall die.

WILLIAM HAZLITT, *TABLE TALK* (1821-1822). ON THE FEAR OF DEATH

. . . . .

Since trifles make the sum of human things,
And half our misery from our foibles springs.

HANNAH MORE (1745-1833), *SENSIBILITY*

. . . . .

Ah! It is well for the unfortunate to be resigned, but for the
guilty there is no peace.

MARY SHELLEY, *FRANKENSTEIN* (1818)

. . . . .

Believe me, if all those endearing young charms
Which I gaze on so fondly today,
Were to change by tomorrow and fleet in my arms,
Like fairy gifts fading away,
Thou would'st still be adored as this moment thou art,
Let thy loveliness fade as it will,
And around the dear ruin each wish of my heart
Would entwine itself verdantly still.

THOMAS MOORE, *IRISH MELODIES* (1807-1834). BELIEVE ME, IF ALL THOSE
ENDEARING YOUNG CHARMS, ST. 1

. . . . .

I am always at a loss to know how much to believe of my own
stories.

WASHINGTON IRVING, *TALES OF A TRAVELER* (1824).

. . . . .

I am not resigned: I am not sure life is long enough to learn
that lesson.

GEORGE ELIOT, *THE MILL ON THE FLOSS* (1860)

. . . . .

Anger and jealousy can no more bear to lose sight of their
objects than love.

GEORGE ELIOT, *THE MILL ON THE FLOSS* (1860)

. . . . .

Success is counted sweetest
By those who ne'er succeed.

EMILY DICKINSON, #67 (WRITTEN C. 1859, PUBLISHED 1878), L. 1

. . . . .

The illusion that times that were are better than those that are,
has probably pervaded all ages.

HORACE GREELEY, *THE AMERICAN CONFLICT* (1864-1866)

. . . . .

Fame is a pearl many dive for and only a few bring up. Even when they do, it is not perfect, and they sigh for more, and lose better things in struggling for them.

LOUISA MAY ALCOTT, *Jo's Boys* (1886)

. . . . .

Nobody knows enough, but many know too much.

MARIE VON EBNER-ESCHENBACH, *Aphorisms* (1893)

. . . . .

Show me one who boasts continually of his "openness," and I will show you one who conceals much.

MINNA THOMAS ANTRIM, *At the Sign of the Golden Calf* (1905)

. . . . .

People do not die for us immediately,
but remain bathed in a sort of aura of life
which bears no relation to true immortality
but through which they continue to occupy our thoughts
as when they were alive.
It is as if they were traveling abroad.

MARCEL PROUST, (C. 1927) *Remembrance of Things Past* (1985)

. . . . .

There is nothing that gives more assurance than a mask.

COLETTE, *My Apprenticeships* (1936)

. . . . .

Some people are molded by their admirations, others by their hostilities.

ELIZABETH BOWEN, *The Death of the Heart* (1938)

. . . . .

The tragedy of life is that people do not change.

AGATHA CHRISTIE, *There Is a Tide* (1948)

. . . . .

When the habitually even-tempered suddenly fly into a
passion, that explosion is apt to be more impressive than the
outburst of the most violent amongst us.

MARGERY ALLINGHAM, *DEATH OF A GHOST* (1934)

. . . . .

It is only in romances that people undergo a sudden
metamorphosis. In real life, even after the most terrible
experiences, the main character remains exactly the same.

ISADORA DUNCAN, *MY LIFE* (1942)

. . . . .

It's not true that life is one damn thing after another—it's one
damn thing over and over.

EDNA ST. VINCENT MILLAY (1930), IN ALLAN ROSS MACDOUGALL, ED.,
LETTERS OF EDNA ST. VINCENT MILLAY (1952)

. . . . .

I'm not frightened of the darkness outside. It's the darkness
inside houses I don't like.

SHELAGH DELANEY, *A TASTE OF HONEY* (1958)

. . . . .

Of one thing alone I am very sure: it is a law of our nature that
the memory of longing should survive the more fugitive
memory of fulfillment.

ELLEN GLASGOW, *THE WOMAN WITHIN* (1954)

. . . . .

So long as one is able to pose one has still much to learn about
suffering.

ELLEN GLASGOW, *LETTERS OF ELLEN GLASGOW* (1958)

. . . . .

It's the most unhappy people who most fear change.

MIGNON MCLAUGHLIN, *THE SECOND NEUROTIC'S NOTEBOOK* (1966)

. . . . .

People who cannot feel punish those who do.

MAY SARTON, *MRS. STEVENS HEARS THE MERMAIDS SINGING* (1965)

. . . . .

The soft-minded man always fears change. He feels security in the status quo, and he has an almost morbid fear of the new. For him, the greatest pain is the pain of a new idea.

MARTIN LUTHER KING, JR., *STRENGTH TO LOVE* (1963)

. . . . .

Now when you hates you shrinks up inside and gets littler and you squeezes your heart tight and you stays so mad with peoples you feels sick all the time like you needs the doctor.

MARGARET WALKER, *JUBILEE* (1966)

. . . . .

In hatred as in love, we grow like the thing we brood upon. What we loathe, we graft into our very soul.

MARY RENAULT, *THE MASK OF APOLLO* (1966)

. . . . .

The movement from certainty to uncertainty is what I call fear . . . . Most of us want to have our minds continually occupied so that we are prevented from seeing ourselves as we actually are. We are afraid to be empty. We are afraid to look at our fears.

J. KRISHNAMURTI, *FREEDOM FROM THE KNOWN* (1969)

. . . . .

My trouble is I analyze life instead of live it.

HUGH PRATHER, *NOTES TO MYSELF* (1979)

. . . . .

Nothing is so dear as what you're about to leave.

JESSAMYN WEST, *THE LIFE I REALLY LIVED* (1979)

. . . . .

But the gates of my happy childhood had clanged shut behind me; I had become adult enough to recognize the need to conceal unbearable emotions for the sake of others.

EVA FIGES, *LITTLE EDEN* (1978)

. . . . .

I am convinced that this anxiety that runs through my life is the tension between what I "should be" and what I am. My anxiety does not come from thinking about the future but from wanting to control it . . . .

HUGH PRATHER, *NOTES TO MYSELF* (1979)

. . . . .

This realization was shattering for all of us. It was so easy to fall into the trap of competing with men instead of living up to one's potential.

SHIRLEY MACLAINE, *YOU CAN GET THERE FROM HERE* (1975)

. . . . .

That was the first time it occurred to me that all my life I had feared imprisonment, the nun's cell, the hospital bed, the places where one faced the self without distraction, without the crutches of other people.

EDNA O'BRIEN, *THE LOVE OBJECT* (1976)

. . . . .

The truth is that we can overhaul our surroundings, renovate our environment, talk a new game, join a new club, far more easily than we can change the way we respond emotionally. It is easier to change behavior than feelings about that behavior.

ELLEN GOODMAN, *TURNING POINTS* (1979)

. . . . .

Two fundamental impulses of grief—to return to the time before death, and to reach forward to a state of mind where the past is forgotten.

PETER MARRIS, *LOSS AND CHANGE* (1974)

．　．　．　．　．

For three days they waited in a purposeless vacuum, Justine in London, Meggie and the family on Drogheda, stretching the official silence into tenuous hope. Oh, surely after so long it would turn out to be a mistake, surely if it was true they would have heard by now! Dane would come in Justine's front door smiling, and say it was all a silly mistake . . . . Dane would come in the door and laugh the idea of his death to scorn, he'd stand there tall and strong and alive, and he'd laugh. Hope began to grow, and grew with every minute they waited. Treacherous, horrible hope. He wasn't dead, no! Not drowned, not Dane who was a good enough swimmer to brave any kind of sea and live. So they waited, not acknowledging what had happened in the hope it would prove to be a mistake.

COLLEEN McCULLOUGH, *THE THORN BIRDS* (1977)

．　．　．　．　．

Hold on to what is good
even if it is
    a handful of earth.
Hold on to what you believe
even if it is
    a tree which stands by itself.
Hold on to what you must do
even if it is
    a long way from here.
Hold on to life
even when
    it is easier to let go.

NANCY WOOD, *MANY WINTERS* (1974)

．　．　．　．　．

How desperately we wish to maintain our trust in those we love! In the face of everything, we try to find reasons to trust. Because losing faith is worse than falling out of love.

SONIA JOHNSON, *FROM HOUSEWIFE TO HERETIC* (1981)

. . . . .

Why is it that people who cannot show feeling presume that that is a strength and not a weakness?

MAY SARTON, *AT SEVENTY: A JOURNAL* (1982-1983)

. . . . .

 Through anger, the truth looks simple.

JANE MCCABE, IN CAROLYN HEILBRUN, *WRITING A WOMAN'S LIFE* (1988)

. . . . .

Many we had worked with who were not in pain had less of a tendency to investigate, had less motivation to examine and begin to let go of their suffering. Because things weren't "so bad after all," they imagined they could somehow hide from death in the same way they had hidden from life.

STEPHEN LEVINE, *WHO DIES? (1989)*

. . . . .

I have a right to my anger, and I don't want anybody telling me I shouldn't be, that it's not nice to be, and that something's wrong with me because I get angry.

MAXINE WATERS, IN Brian Lanker, *I DREAM A WORLD (1989)*

. . . . .

 Of all human activities, none is so useless and potentially destructive as trying to predict the future. The future is merely a shadow which blocks out the joys of the present and emphasizes the miseries of the past.

ERICA JONG, *HOW TO SAVE YOUR OWN LIFE* (1995)

Letting Go

.   .   .   .   .

Eye for eye, tooth for tooth,
hand for hand, foot for foot.

EXODUS 21:24

.   .   .   .   .

. . . a man hath no better thing under the sun,
than to eat, and to drink, and to be merry.

ECCLESIASTES 8:15

.   .   .   .   .

She [Helen] threw into the wine which they were drinking
a drug which takes away grief and passion
and brings forgetfulness of all ills.

HOMER (C. 700 B.C.), THE ODYSSEY, BK. IV, L. 220

.   .   .   .   .

The loss which is unknown is no loss at all.

PUBLILIUS SYRUS (1ST CENTURY B.C.), MAXIM 38

.   .   .   .   .

Abandon learning and there will be no sorrow.

LAO-TZU (C. 604-C. 531 B.C.), THE WAY OF LAO-TZU, 20

.   .   .   .   .

He that conceals his grief
finds no remedy for it.

TURKISH PROVERB

. . . . .

Each man for hymself.

GEOFFREY CHAUCER, "THE KNIGHT'S TALE, L," (1182), THE CANTERBURY TALES (C. 1387)

. . . . .

And when he is out of sight, quickly also is he out of mind.

THOMAS À KEMPIS, IMITATION OF CHRIST (C. 1420)

. . . . .

Absense, that common cure of love.

MIGUEL DE CERVANTES, DON QUIXOTE DE LA MANCHA (1605-1615)

. . . . .

Since there's no help, come let us kill and part —
Nay, I have done: you get no more of me,
And I am glad, yea glad with all my heart,
That thus so cleanly I myself can free.
Shake hands forever, cancel all our vows,
And when we meet at any time again,
Be it not seen in either of our brows
That we one jot of former love retain.

MICHEAL DRAYTON, POEMS (1619)

. . . . .

There is no man so good, who, were he to submit all his thoughts and actions to the laws, would not deserve hanging ten times in his life.

MICHEL EYQUEM DE MONTAIGNE, ESSAYS (1595)

. . . . .

For gnarling sorrow hath less power to bite
The man that mocks at it and sets it light.

WILLIAM SHAKESPEARE, KING RICHARD THE SECOND (1595), ACT I, SC. III, L. 292

. . . . .

For I am nothing if not critical.

WILLIAM SHAKESPEARE, OTHELLO (1604-1605), ACT II, SC. I, L. 119

. . . . .

I had rather have a fool to make me merry than experience to make me sad.

WILLIAM SHAKESPEARE, *As You Like It* (1599-1600), ACT IV, SC. I, L. 28

. . . . .

All my joys to this are folly,
Naught so sweet as melancholy.

ROBERT BURTON, *The Anatomy of Melancholy* (1621-1651)

. . . . .

Our doubts are traitors,
And make us lose the good we oft might win,
By fearing to attempt.

WILLIAM SHAKESPEARE, MEASURE FOR MEASURE (1604), ACT I, SC. IV, L. 78

. . . . .

To show an unfelt sorrow is an office
Which the false man does easy.

WILLIAM SHAKESPEARE, *Macbeth* (1606), ACT II, SC. III, L. 143

. . . . .

Few love to hear the sins they love to act.

WILLIAM SHAKESPEARE, *Coriolanus* (1607-1608), ACT I, SC. I, L. 92

. . . . .

Ah! do not, when my heart hath 'scap'd this sorrow,
Come in the rearward of a conquer'd woe;
Give not a windy night a rainy morrow,
To linger out a purpos'd overthrow.

WILLIAM SHAKESPEARE, *Sonnet 90* (PUBLISHED 1609), L. 5

. . . . .

It is a heretic that makes the fire,
Not she which burn in 't.

WILLIAM SHAKESPEARE, *The Winter's Tale* (1610-1611), ACT II, SC. III, L. 115

．　．　．　．　．

She should have died hereafter;
There would have been a time for such a word.
Tomorrow, and tomorrow, and tomorrow,
Creeps in this pretty pace from day to day,
To the last syllable of recorded time;
And all our yesterdays have lighted fools
The way to dusty death. Out, out, brief candle!
Life's but a walking shadow, a poor player
That struts and frets his hour upon the stage,
And then is heard no more; it is a tale
Told by an idiot, full of sound and fury,
Signifying nothing.

WILLIAM SHAKESPEARE, *MACBETH* (1606), ACT V, SC. V, L. 17

．　．　．　．　．

Heart,
I told you before and twice, and then three times,
don't knock at that door.
No one will answer.

SPANISH FOLK SONG

．　．　．　．　．

Oh do not die, for I shall hate
All women so, when thou art gone.

JOHN DONNE (1572-1631), *A FEVER*, ST. 1

．　．　．　．　．

Vain the ambitions of kings
Who seek by trophies and dead things
To leave a living name behind,
And weave but nets to catch the wind.

JOHN WEBSTER, "THE DEVIL'S LAW CASE" (1623), SONG

．　．　．　．　．

Whose house is of glass, must not throw stones at another.

GEORGE HERBERT, *JACULA PRUDENTUM* (1651), NO. 196

.   .   .   .   .

Every one that flatters thee
Is no friend in misery.
Words are easy, like the wind;
Faithful friends are hard to find.
Every man will be thy friend
Whilst thou hast wherewith to spend;
But if store of crowns be scant,
No man will supply thy want.

RICHARD BARNFIELD, "ODE," *POEMS: IN DIVERS HUMOURS* (1598)

.   .   .   .   .

The heart of man is the place the devils dwell in:
I feel sometimes a hell within myself.

SIR THOMAS BROWNE, *RELIGIO MEDICI* (1642), PT. I, SEC. 51

.   .   .   .   .

We all have strength enough to endure the misfortunes of
others.

FRANÇOIS, DUC DE LA ROCHEFOUCAULD, *REFLECTIONS; OR, SENTENCES AND
MORAL MAXIMS* (1678), MAXIM 19

.   .   .   .   .

If we had no faults of our own, we would not take so much
pleasure in noticing those of others.

FRANÇOIS, DUC DE LA ROCHEFOUCAULD, *REFLECTIONS; OR, SENTENCES AND
MORAL MAXIMS* (1678), MAXIM 31

.   .   .   .   .

There are very few people who are not ashamed of having been
in love when they no longer love each other.

FRANÇOIS, DUC DE LA ROCHEFOUCAULD, *REFLECTIONS; OR, SENTENCES AND
MORAL MAXIMS* (1678), MAXIM 71

.   .   .   .   .

Hypocrisy is the homage that vice pays to virtue.

FRANÇOIS, DUC DE LA ROCHEFOUCAULD, *REFLECTIONS; OR, SENTENCES AND
MORAL MAXIMS* (1678), MAXIM 218

. . . . .

Doubts are more cruel than the worst of truths.

MOLIÉRE (JEAN BAPTISTE POQUELIN), *LE MISANTHROPE* (1666), ACT III, SC. VII

. . . . .

Of all the griefs that harass the distrest,
sure the most bitter is a scornful jest.

SAMUEL JOHNSON, *LONDON* (1738) (AN IMITATION OF THE THIRD SATIRE OF
JUVENAL), L. 166

. . . . .

A gentleman who had been very unhappy in marriage, married
immediately after his wife died: Johnson said, it was the
triumph of hope over experience.

SAMUEL JOHNSON, IN *BOSWELL, LIFE OF JOHNSON*, JULY 21, 1770

. . . . .

I would rather be attacked than unnoticed. For the worst thing
you can do to an author is to be silent as to his works.

SAMUEL JOHNSON, IN *BOSWELL, LIFE OF JOHNSON*, MARCH 26, 1779

. . . . .

To each his suff'rings: all are men,
Condemn'd alike to groan,
The tender for another's pain,
Th' unfeeling for his own.
Yet ah! why should they know their fate,
Since sorrow never comes too late,
And happiness too swiftly flies?
Thought would destroy their paradise.
No more; where ignorance is bliss,
'Tis folly to be wise.

THOMAS GRAY, *ON A DISTANT PROSPECT OF ETON COLLEGE* (1742), ST. 10

. . . . .

A useless life is an early death.

JOHANN WOLFGANG VON GOETHE, *IPHIGENIA IN TAURIS* (1787), ACT I, SC. II

. . . . .

When my mother died I was very young,
And my father sold me while yet my tongue
Could scarcely cry "'weep!'weep!'weep!"
So your chimneys I sweep, and in soot I sleep.

WILLIAM BLAKE, "THE CHIMNEY SWEEPER," SONGS OF INNOCENCE (1789), ST. 1

. . . . .

You saw his weakness, and he will never forgive you.

JOHANN CHRISTOPH FRIEDRICH VON SCHILLER, WILHELM TELL (1804), ACT
III, SC. I

. . . . .

You will be damned if you do.—
And you will be damned if you don't [definition of Calvinism].

LORENZO DOW (1777-1834), REFLECTIONS ON THE LOVE OF GOD

. . . . .

Wit lasts no more than two centuries.

STENDHAL (HENRI BEYLE), REPLY TO BALZAC (OCTOBER 30, 1840)

. . . . .

There is nobody who is not dangerous for someone.

MARIE DE RABUTIN-CHANTAL, MARQUISE DE SÉVIGNÉ LETTERS OF MADAME DE
SÉVIGNÉ TO HER DAUGHTER AND HER FRIENDS (1811)

. . . . .

I am not at all the sort of person you and I took me for.

JANE WELSH CARLYLE, "LETTER TO THOMAS CARLYLE (1822)," IN ALAN AND
MARY MCQUEEN SIMPSON, EDS., I TOO AM HERE (1977)

. . . . .

What the eye does not see, the heart does not grieve.

DANISH SAYING

. . . . .

Cynicism is an unpleasant way of saying the truth.

LILLIAN HELLMAN, THE LITTLE FOXES (1939)

Breathes there the man, with soul so dead,
Who never to himself hath said,
This is my own, my native land!
Whose heart hath ne'er within him burn'd
As home his footsteps he hath turn'd
From wandering on a foreign strand!
If such there breathe, go, mark him well;
For him no Minstrel raptures swell;
High though his titles, proud his name,
Boundless his wealth as wish can claim;
Despite those titles, power, and pelf,
The wretch, concentered all in self,
Living, shall forfeit fair renown,
And, doubly dying, shall go down
To the vile dust, from whence he sprung,
Unwept, unhonor'd, and unsung.

SIR WALTER SCOTT, *THE LAY OF THE LAST MISTREL* (1805), CANTO VI, ST. 1

Life is only error,
And death is knowledge.

JOHANN CHRISTOPH FRIEDRICH VON SCHILLER, *CASSANDRA (1802)*

You are discontented with the world because you can't get just
the small things that suit your pleasure, not because it's a world
where myriads of men and women are ground by wrong and
misery, and tainted with pollution.

GEORGE ELIOT, FELIX HOLT, *THE RADICAL* (1866)

The longest absence is less perilous to love
than the terrible trials of incessant proximity.

OUIDA, WISDOM, WIT AND PATHOS (1884)

. . . . .

How happy are the pessimists!
What joy is theirs when they have proved that there is no joy.

MARIE VON EBNER-ESCHENBACH, *APHORISMS* (1893)

. . . . .

Life is an illusion.

MATA HARI, 1917, IN BARBARA McDOWELL AND HANA UMLAUF, *WOMAN'S ALMANAC* (1977), AS SHE PREPARED TO MEET FIRING SQUAD.

. . . . .

Science may have found a cure for most evils; but it has found no remedy for the worst of them all—the apathy of human beings.

HELEN KELLER, *MY RELIGION* (1927)

. . . . .

What we call mourning for our dead is perhaps
not so much grief at not being able to call them back
as it is grief at not being able to want to do so.

THOMAS MANN, *THE MAGIC MOUNTAIN* (1924)

. . . . .

Fond as we are of our loved ones,
there comes at times during their absence an unexplained peace.

ANNE SHAW, *BUT SUCH IS LIFE* (1931)

. . . . .

I warn you . . . I am only really myself when I'm somebody else whom I have endowed with these wonderful qualities from my imagination.

ZELDA FITZGERALD, *SAVE ME THE WALTZ* (1932)

. . . . .

It doesn't pay well to fight for what we believe in.

LILLIAN HELLMAN, *WATCH ON THE RHINE* (1941)

．　．　．　．　．

When you are unhappy or dissatisfied,
is there anything in the world more maddening than to be told
that you should be contented with your lot?

KATHLEEN NORRIS, *HANDS FULL OF LIVING* (1931)

．　．　．　．　．

Good-byes breed a sort of distaste for whomever you say good-
bye to; this hurts, you feel, this must not happen again.

ELIZABETH BOWEN, *THE HOUSE IN PARIS* (1935)

．　．　．　．　．

He acted too often without counting the cost, from some
dazzling conception—one could not say from impulse, for
impulses are from the heart. He liked to reorganize and change
things for the sake of change, to make a fine gesture. He
destroyed the old before he had clearly thought out the new.

WILLA CATHER, *SHADOWS ON THE ROCK* (1931)

．　．　．　．　．

He hated people who reeled off their thoughts and feelings to
you, who took it for granted that you wanted to know their
inner mechanism. Reserve was always more interesting.

AGATHA CHRISTIE, *SAD CYPRESS* (1939)

．　．　．　．　．

Avoiding danger is no safer in the long run than outright
exposure. The fearful are caught as often as the bold.

HELEN KELLER, *LET US HAVE FAITH* (1940)

．　．　．　．　．

The things people discard tell more about them than the
things they keep.

HILDA LAWRENCE, *THE PAVILION* (1946)

．　．　．　．　．

The more hidden the venom, the more dangerous it is.

MARGUERITE DE VALOIS, *FROM FRENCH WIT AND WISDOM* (1950)

. . . . .

Lonely people talking to each other can make each other lonelier.

LILLIAN HELLMAN, *The Autumn Garden* (1951)

. . . . .

Mrs. Hopewell had no bad qualities of her own but she was able to use other people's in such a constructive way that she never felt the lack.

FLANNERY O'CONNOR, *A Good Man Is Hard to Find* (1953)

. . . . .

We are such stuff as manure is made on, so let's drink up and forget it.

EUGENE O'NEILL, *Long Day's Journey Into Night* (1956)

. . . . .

People change and forget to tell each other.

LILLIAN HELLMAN, *Toys in the Attic* (1960)

. . . . .

Didn't you ever notice how it's always people who wish they had somethin' or had done somethin' that hate the hardest?

GRACE METALIOUS, *Peyton Place* (1956)

. . . . .

Go, go, go, said the bird: human kind
Cannot bear very much reality.

T. S. ELIOT, FROM *Burnt Norton*, IN *The Complete Poems and Plays* (1958), L. 44

. . . . .

Even though a number of people have tried, no one has yet found a way to drink for a living.

JEAN KERR, *Poor Richard* (1965)

. . . . .

Dwelling on the negative simply contributes to its power.

SHIRLEY MACLAINE, OUT ON A LIMB (1983)

. . . . .

Mayo was anxious to leave and like so many enthusiasts seemed liable to turn a social escape into a jail break if anything threatened to hinder him.

MARGERY ALLINGHAM, THE MIND READERS (1965)

. . . . .

Failure can get to be a rather comfortable old friend.

MIGNON MCLAUGHLIN, THE SECOND NEUROTIC'S NOTEBOOK (1966)

. . . . .

He has destroyed his talent himself—by not using it, by betrayals of himself and what he believed in, by drinking so much that he blunted the edge of his perceptions, by laziness, by sloth, by snobbery; by hook and by crook; selling vitality, trading it for security, for comfort.

ERNEST HEMINGWAY, THE SNOWS OF KILIMANJARO (1964)

. . . . .

Amnesty: an act by which sovereigns commonly pardon injustices committed by themselves.

ANONYMOUS, GRAFFITO WRITTEN DURING FRENCH STUDENT REVOLT (1968)

. . . . .

You come into the world alone and you go out of the world alone yet it seems to me you are more alone while living than even going and coming.

EMILY CARR, HUNDREDS AND THOUSANDS (1966)

. . . . .

He was in the grip of that most trying form of depression— the melancholy of enforced inaction.

PATRICIA MOYES, DOWN AMONG THE DEAD MEN (1961)

. . . . .

One more drink and I'd have been under the host.

DOROTHY PARKER (1930), IN HOWARD TEICHMANN, *GEORGE S. KAUFMAN*
(1972)

. . . . .

Is it age, or was it always my nature, to take a bad time, block
out the good times, until any success became an accident,
failure seemed the only truth?

LILLIAN HELLMAN, *AN UNFINISHED WOMAN* (1969)

. . . . .

It seems to me you can be awfully happy in this life if you
stand aside and watch and mind your own business, and let
other people do as they like about damaging themselves and
one another. You go on kidding yourself that you're impartial
and tolerant and all that, then all of a sudden you realize you're
dead, and you've never been alive at all.

MARY STEWART, *THIS ROUGH MAGIC* (1964)

. . . . .

We are the unwilling,
led by the unqualified,
doing the unnecessary,
for the ungrateful.

Anonymous GRAFFITO, AMERICAN AIR BASE, VIETNAM (1970)

. . . . .

We are able to laugh when we achieve detachment, if only for a
moment.

MAY SARTON, JOURNAL OF A SOLITUDE (1973)

. . . . .

Of all the tyrannies which have usurped power over humanity,
few have been able to enslave the mind and body as
imperiously as drug addiction.

FREDA ADLER, *SISTERS IN CRIME* (1975)

. . . . .

When I spoke of having a drink, it was a euphemism for
having a whole flock of them.

MARGARET HALSEY, *NO LAUGHING MATTER* (1977)

. . . . .

Detached I feel
apart from people
an onlooker.
I want to feel in the mainstream
a part of
not apart from.
To cross the charm is the goal.
To feel a part of the whole
allows the freedom to be apart from
and still a part of.

THETA BURKE, *I'VE HEARD YOUR FEELINGS* (1976)

. . . . .

To be alone is to be different,
to be different is to be alone.

SUZANNE GORDON, *LONELY IN AMERICA* (1976)

. . . . .

My old flame,
I can't even think of his name.

POPULAR SONG (1970s)

. . . . .

If we do not know how to mourn, we cannot know how to live;
and the diffuse distress of unacknowledged grief will destroy
our liberalism and our respect for life.

PETER MARRIS, *LOSS AND CHANGE* (1974)

. . . . .

I'm doing well, especially since I moved away from here.

JUDY GRAHN, *THE QUEEN OF SWORDS* (1987)

Alcoholism isn't a spectator sport.
Eventually the whole family gets to play.

JOYCE REBETA-BURDITT, *THE CRACKER FACTORY* (1977)

When you don't know when you have been spit on, it does not matter too much what else you think you know.

RUTH SHAYS, IN JOHN LANGSTON GWALTNEY, *DRYLONGSO* (1980)

I personally think we developed language because of our deep need to complain.

JANE WAGNER, *THE SEARCH FOR SIGNS OF INTELLIGENT LIFE IN THE UNIVERSE* (1985)

Cynicism is more than a pose; it's also a handy time saver. By deflating your companion's enthusiasm, you can cut conversations in half.

LISA BIRNBACH, *THE OFFICIAL PREPPY HANDBOOK* (1980)

Alcohol doesn't console, it doesn't fill up anyone's psychological gaps, all it replaces is the lack of God.

MARGUERITE DURAS, *PRACTICALITIES* (1987)

One sank into the ancient sin of anomie when challenges failed.

AMANDA CROSS, *DEATH IN A TENURED POSITION* (1981)

A cynical young person is almost the saddest sight to see, because it means that *he or she has gone from knowing nothing to believing in nothing.*

MAYA ANGELOU, IN BRIAN LANKER, *I DREAM A WORLD* (1989)

. . . . .

He . . . treats his emotions like mice that infest our basement or the rats in the garage, as vermin to be crushed in traps or poisoned with bait.

MARGE PIERCY, *BRAIDED LIVES* (1982)

. . . . .

I did not lose myself all at once. I rubbed out my face over the years washing away my pain, the same way carvings on stone are worn down by water.

AMY TAN, *THE JOY LUCK CLUB* (1989)

. . . . .

Divorce is the one human tragedy that reduces everything to cash.

RITA MAE BROWN, *SUDDEN DEATH* (1983)

. . . . .

Like many people in personal turmoil, she rose late, didn't dress other than to cloak herself in her dressing gown, and she fell asleep easily throughout the day.

CAROL BLY, *BACKBONE* (1982)

. . . . .

What stops you killing yourself when you're intoxicated out of your mind is the thought that once you're dead you won't be able to drink any more.

MARGUERITE DURAS, *PRACTICALITIES* (1987)

. . . . .

He searched for his accustomed fear of death and could not find it.

LEO TOLSTOY, *THE DEATH OF IVAN ILYICH* (1886)

Becoming Aware

. . . . .

Out of the depths have I cried unto thee, O Lord.
Lord, hear my voice:
Let thine ears be attentive to the voice of my supplications.
If thou, Lord, shouldest mark iniquities,
O Lord, who shall stand?
But *there is* forgiveness with thee, that thou mayest be feared.

> PSALM 130:1-4

. . . . .

The deeper the sorrow, the less tongue it has.

> THE TALMUD (COMPILED C. 6TH CENTURY A.D.)

. . . . .

Even in laughter the heart is sorrowful.

> PROVERBS 14:13

. . . . .

For the thing which I greatly feared is come and that which I
was afraid of is come unto me. I was not in safety, neither had I
rest, neither was I quiet; yet trouble came.

> JOB 3:25-26

. . . . .

Is it nothing to you, all ye that pass by?
behold, and see if there be any sorrow like unto my sorrow.

> LAMENTATIONS 1:12

.   .   .   .   .

The Moon and Pleiades have set,
Midnight is nigh,
The time is passing, passing, yet
Alone I lie.

> SAPPHO (C. 612 B.C.), IN C. R. HAINES, ED., SAPPHO: *THE POEMS AND*
> *FRAGMENTS (1926)*

.   .   .   .   .

He who knows does not speak.
He who speaks does not know.

> LAO-TZU (C. 604-C. 531 B.C.), *THE WAY OF LAO-TZU, 56*

.   .   .   .   .

What restraint or limit should there be to grief for one so
dear?

> HORACE, *ODES*, BK. I, ODE XXIV, 1

.   .   .   .   .

Grief teaches the steadiest minds to waver.

> SOPHOCLES, *ANTIGONE* (C. 442 B.C.), L. 563

.   .   .   .   .

Death is not the worst; rather, in vain
To wish for death, and not to compass it.

> SOPHOCLES (C. 495-406 B.C.), *ELECTRA, L. 1008*

.   .   .   .   .

What greater grief than the loss of one's native land.

> EURIPIDES, *MEDEA* (431 B.C.), L. 650

.   .   .   .   .

The life which is unexamined is not worth living.

> PLATO (C. 428-348 B.C.), *DIALOGUES, APOLOGY, 38*

.   .   .   .   .

I was shipwrecked before I got aboard.

> LUCIUS ANNAEUS SENECA (C. 4 B.C.-A.D. 65), *EPISTLES 87, 1*

. . . . .

When life is so burdensome,
death has become for a man a sought-after refuge.

HERODOTUS (C. 485-C. 425 B.C.), *THE HISTORIES OF HERODOTUS*, BK. VII, CH. 46

. . . . .

He truly sorrows who sorrows unseen.

MARTIAL, *EPIGRAMS* (86 A.D.)

. . . . .

Emptied with weeping
my eyes are
two buckets of the waterman
as he walks among orchard trees.

SAFIYA BINT MUSAFIR, IN JOANNA BANKIER AND DEIRDRE LASHGARI, EDS.,
WOMEN POETS OF THE WORLD (1983). "AT THE BADR TRENCH" (7TH CENTURY)

. . . . .

There is no greater sorrow
Than to be mindful of the happy time
In misery.

DANTE ALIGHIERI, *THE DIVINE COMEDY* (C. 1310-1321). INFERNO, CANTO V, L. 121

. . . . .

You cannot see the wood for the trees.

JOHN HEYWOOD, PROVERBS (1546), PT. II, CH. 4

. . . . .

Twill grieve me so to the heart that I shall cry my eyes out.

MIGUEL DE CERVANTES, *DON QUIXOTE DE LA MANCHA* (1605-1615)

. . . . .

Sorrow breaks seasons and reposing hours,
Makes the night morning, and the noontide night.

WILLIAM SHAKESPEARE, *KING RICHARD THE THIRD* (1592-1593), ACT I, SC. IV, L. 76

. . . . .

Farewell, thou child of my right hand, and joy!
My sin was too much hope of thee, lov'd boy.

BEN JONSON, ON MY FIRST SON (WRITTEN C. 1603), IN EPIGRAMS (1616)

. . . . .

Affliction may one day smile again;
and till then, sit thee down, sorrow!

WILLIAM SHAKESPEARE, LOVE'S LABOUR'S LOST (1594-1595), ACT I, SC. I, L. 312

. . . . .

No man is born unto himself alone;
Who lives unto himself, he lives to none.

FRANCIS QUARLES, ESTHER (1621), SEC. 1, MEDITATION 1

. . . . .

I will instruct my sorrows to be proud;
For grief is proud and makes his owner stoop.

WILLIAM SHAKESPEARE, KING JOHN (1594-1596), ACT III, SC. I, L. 68

. . . . .

Was there ever a grief like mine?

GEORGE HERBERT, THE TEMPLE (1633). THE CHURCH. THE SACRIFICE, REFRAIN

. . . . .

Call in thy death's head there: tie up thy fears.

GEORGE HERBERT, THE TEMPLE (1633). THE COLLAR

. . . . .

Each substance of a grief hath twenty shadows.

WILLIAM SHAKESPEARE, KING RICHARD THE SECOND (1595), ACT II, SC. II, L. 14

. . . . .

For want of a nail the shoe is lost,
for want of a shoe the horse is lost,
for want of a horse the rider is lost.

GEORGE HERBERT, JACULA PRUDENTUM (1651), NO. 499

. . . . .

All my pretty ones?
Did you say all? O hell-kite! All? But I must also feel it as a
man:
I cannot but remember such things were,
That were most precious to me.

WILLIAM SHAKESPEARE, *MACBETH* (1606), ACT IV, SC. III, L. 216-219

. . . . .

O! that I were as great
As is my grief, or lesser than my name,
Or that I could forget what I have been,
Or not remember what I must be now.

WILLIAM SHAKESPEARE, *KING RICHARD THE SECOND* (1595), ACT III, SC. III, L. 136

. . . . .

When sorrows come, they come not single spies,
But in battalions.

WILLIAM SHAKESPEARE, *HAMLET* (1600-1601), ACT IV, SC. V, L. 78

. . . . .

No man can lose what he never had.

IZAAK WALTON, *THE COMPLEAT ANGLER* (1653-1655). EPISTLE TO THE
READER, PT. I, CH

. . . . .

My joy, my grief, my hope, my love,
Did all within this circle move!

EDMUND WALLER, *ON A GIRDLE* (1664), ST. 2

. . . . .

When I consider how my light is spent,
Ere half my days, in this dark world and wide,
And that one talent which is death to hide
Lodg'd with me useless.

JOHN MILTON, *ON HIS BLINDNESS* (1652)

Come away, come away, death,
And in sad cypress let me be laid;
Fly away, fly away, breath;
I am slain by a fair cruel maid.

WILLIAM SHAKESPEARE, *TWELFTH-NIGHT* (1601-1602), ACT II, SC. IV, L. 51

If I must die,
I will encounter darkness as a bride,
And hug it in my arms.

WILLIAM SHAKESPEARE, *MEASURE FOR MEASURE* (1604), ACT III, SC. I, L. 81

The seat of desolation, void of light.

JOHN MILTON, *PARADISE LOST* (1667) BK. I, L. 181

If it were now to die,
'Twere now to be most happy.

WILLIAM SHAKESPEARE, *OTHELLO* (1604-1605), ACT II, SC. I, L. 192

Long is the way
And hard, that out of hell leads up to light.

JOHN MILTON, *PARADISE LOST* (1667) BK. II, L. 432

The worst is not,
So long as we can say, "This is the worst."

WILLIAM SHAKESPEARE, *KING LEAR* (1605), ACT IV, SC. I, L. 27

Reputation, reputation, reputation!
O! I have lost my reputation.
I have lost the immortal part of myself,
and what remains is bestial.

WILLIAM SHAKESPEARE, *OTHELLO* (1604-1605), ACT II, SC. III, L. 264

. . . . .

For who would lose,
Though full of pain, this intellectual being,
Those thoughts that wander through eternity,
To perish rather, swallow'd up and lost
In the wide womb of uncreated night,
Devoid of sense and motion?

JOHN MILTON, *PARADISE LOST* (1667) BK. II, L. 146

. . . . .

Me miserable! which way shall I fly
Infinite wrath, and infinite despair?
Which way I fly is hell; myself am hell;
And in the lowest deep a lower deep,
Still threat'ning to devour me, opens wide,
To which the hell I suffer seems a heaven.

JOHN MILTON, *PARADISE LOST* (1667) BK. IV, L. 73

. . . . .

The weight of this sad time we must obey;
Speak what we feel, not what we ought to say.

WILLIAM SHAKESPEARE, *KING LEAR* (1605), ACT V, SC. III, L. 325

. . . . .

So farewell hope, and with hope farewell fear,
Farewell remorse: all good to me is lost;
Evil, be thou my good.

JOHN MILTON, *PARADISE LOST* (1667) BK. IV, L. 108

. . . . .

Dark, dark, dark, amid the blaze of noon,
Irrecoverably dark, total eclipse
Without all hope of day!

JOHN MILTON, *SAMSON AGONISTES* (1671), L. 80

· · · · ·

Show his eyes, and grieve his heart;
Come like shadows, so depart.

WILLIAM SHAKESPEARE, *MACBETH* (1606), ACT IV, SC. I, L. 110

· · · · ·

A mighty pain to love it is,
And 'tis a pain that pain to miss;
But of all pains, the greatest pain
It is to love, but love in vain.

ABRAHAM COWLEY, *ANACREON* (1656), VII, GOLD

· · · · ·

I follow'd rest:
rest fled and soon forsook me;
I ran from grief;
grief ran and overtook me.

FRANCIS QUARLES, *EMBLEMS (1635)*

· · · · ·

Well, everyone can master a
grief but he that has it.

WILLIAM SHAKESPEARE, *MUCH ADO ABOUT NOTHING* (1598-1600), ACT III, SC. II, L. 28

· · · · ·

Tir'd with all these,
for restful death I cry . . .
Tir'd with all these, from these would I be gone,
Save that to die, I leave my love alone.

WILLIAM SHAKESPEARE, *SONNET 66* (PUBLISHED 1609)

· · · · ·

We have left undone those things which we ought to have done;
And we have done those things which we ought not to have done.

MORNING PRAYER, "A GENERAL CONFESSION," FROM *THE BOOK OF COMMON PRAYER* (1706)

. . . . .

When I have seen by Time's fell hand defaced
The rich proud cost of outworn buried age;
When sometime lofty towers I see downrased,
And brass eternal slave to mortal rage;
When I have seen the hungry ocean gain
Advantage on the kingdom of the shore,
And the firm soil win of the wat'ry main,
Increasing store with loss, and loss with store;
When I have seen such interchange of state,
Or state itself confounded to decay,
Ruin hath taught me thus to ruminate,
That Time will come and take my love away.
This thought is as a death, which cannot choose
But weep to have that which it fears to lose.

WILLIAM SHAKESPEARE, *SONNET 64* (PUBLISHED 1609)

. . . . .

My dear mother, sisters and brothers comforted me, but their comfort only increased my sorrow and poured more oil on the fire, so that the flames grew ever higher.

GLUCKEL OF HAMELN, *MEMOIRS OF GLUCKEL OF HAMELN* (1724)

. . . . .

The curfew tolls the knell of parting day,
The lowing herd wind slowly o'er the lea,
The plowman homeward plods his weary way,
And leaves the world to darkness and to me.

THOMAS GRAY, *ELEGY WRITTEN IN A COUNTRY CHURCHYARD* (1750), ST. 1

. . . . .

These are the times that try men's souls.

THOMAS PAINE, *THE AMERICAN CRISIS, NO. 1* (DECEMBER 23, 1776)

. . . . .

But to see her was to love her,
Love but her, and love forever.
Had we never lov'd sae kindly,
Had we never lov'd sae blindly,
Never met nor never parted
We had ne'er been brokenhearted.

ROBERT BURNS, JOHNSON'S MUSICAL MUSEUM (1787-1796)

. . . . .

Alone, alone, all, all alone;
Alone on a wide, wide sea.

SAMUEL TAYLOR COLERIDGE, THE RIME OF THE ANCIENT MARINER (1798), PT. IV, ST. 3

. . . . .

She lived unknown, and few could know
When Lucy ceased to be;
But she is in her grave, and, oh,
The difference to me!

WILLIAM WORDSWORTH, LUCY: SHE DWELT AMONG THE UNTRODDEN WAYS (1799)

. . . . .

I tell you hopeless grief is passionless.

ELIZABETH BARRETT BROWNING, GRIEF, POEMS (1844)

. . . . .

There is no despair so absolute as that which comes with the first moments of our first great sorrow, when we have not yet known what it is to have suffered and to be healed, to have despaired and recovered hope.

GEORGE ELIOT, ADAM BEDE (1859)

. . . . .

I am never afraid of what I know.

ANNA SEWELL, BLACK BEAUTY (1877)

.   .   .   .   .

Ah woe is me! Winter is come and gone,
But grief returns with the revolving year;
The airs and streams renew their joyous tone;
The ants, the bees, the swallows, reappear;
Fresh leaves and flowers deck the dead Seasons' bier;
the amorous birds now pair in every brake,
And build their mossy homes in field and brere;
And the green lizard and the golden snake,
Like unimprisoned flames, out of their trance awake.

Alas! that all we loved of him should be,
But for our grief, as if it had not been,
And grief itself be mortal! Woe is me!
Whence are we, and why are we? of what scene
The actors or spectators? Great and mean
Meet massed in death, who lends what life must borrow.
As long as skies are blue and fields are green,
Evening must usher night, night urge the morrow,
Months follow month with woe, and year wake year to sorrow.

Percy Bysshe Shelley, *Adonais* (1821), st. XVIII and XXI

.   .   .   .   .

There is much pain that is quite noiseless;
and vibrations that make human agonies are often a mere
whisper
in the roar of hurrying existence.

George Eliot, *Felix Holt, the Radical* (1866)

.   .   .   .   .

Life, struck sharp on death,
Makes awful lightning.

Elizabeth Barrett Browning, *Aurora Leigh* (1857), bk. I, l. 210

．　．　．　．　．

Once upon a midnight dreary, while I pondered,
weak and weary,
Over many a quaint and curious volume
of forgotten lore
While I nodded, nearly napping, suddenly
there come a tapping,
As of some one gently rapping, rapping at my chamber door . . . .

Ah, distinctly I remember it was in the
bleak December;
And each separate dying ember
wrought its ghost upon the floor . . . .

Deep into that darkness peering, long I stood
there, wondering, fearing,
Doubting, dreaming dreams no mortal ever dared to
dream before.

EDGAR ALLEN POE, FROM THE RAVEN (1845), ST. 1, 2, 5

．　．　．　．　．

Below the surface stream, shallow and light,
Of what we say and feel—below the stream,
A light, of what we think we feel, there flows
With noiseless current, strong, obscure and deep,
The central stream of what we feel indeed.

MATTHEW ARNOLD, ST. PAUL AND PROTESTANTISM (1870)

．　．　．　．　．

Real sorrow is incompatible with hope.
No matter how great that sorrow may be,
hope raises it one hundred cubits higher.

COMTE DE LAUTREAMONT, POESIES (1870)

．　．　．　．　．

My soul is a broken field plowed by pain.

SARA TEASDALE, FLAME AND SHADOW THE BROKEN FIELD (1920)

. . . . .

The effect corresponding to melancholia is mourning or grief
That is, longing for something that is lost.

Sigmund Freud, *Mourning and Melancholia* (1917)

. . . . .

Fame always brings loneliness.
Success is as ice cold and as lonely as the north pole.

Vicki Baum, *Grand Hotel* (1929)

. . . . .

Death, be not proud, though some have called thee
Mighty and dreadful, for thou are not so:
For those whom thou think'st thou dost overthrow
Die not, poor Death; nor yet canst thou kill me.
From Rest and Sleep, which but thy picture be,
Much pleasure, then from thee much more must flow;
And soonest our best men with thee do go
Rest of their bones and souls' delivery!
Thou'rt slave to fate, chance, kings, and desperate men,
And dost with poison, war, and sickness dwell;
And poppy or charms can make us sleep as well
And better than thy stroke. Why swell'st thou then?
One short sleep past, we wake eternally,
And Death shall be no more: Death, thou shalt die!

John Donne, "Death Be Not Proud," from the *Home Book of Modern Verse* (1953)

. . . . .

All My Sad Captains
I am full of the sorrow that goes with changes in surroundings,
those successive stages of annihilation
that slowly lead to the great and final void.

Isabelle Eberhardt (1900), in Nina De Voogd, tr., *The Passionate Nomad* (1988)

. . . . .

The longed-for ship
Come empty home or founder on the deep,
And eyes first lose their tears and then their sleep.

EDITH WHARTON, *ARTEMIS TO ACTAEON* (1909)

. . . . .

It takes time for the absent
to assume their true shape in our thoughts.

COLETTE, *SIDO* (1930)

. . . . .

It was the last night before sorrow touched her life; and no life
is ever quite the same again when once that cold, sanctifying
touch has been laid upon it.

L. M. MONTGOMERY, *ANNE OF GREEN GABLES* (1908)

. . . . .

We wasters of sorrows!
How we stare away into sad endurance beyond them,
tryng to foresee their end!
Whereas they are nothing else
than our winter foliage, our sombre evergreen,
one of the seasons of our interiour year.

RAINER MARIA RILKE, *THE TENTH ELEGY* (1923)

. . . . .

How cold to the living hour grief could make you!

EUDORA WELTY, *THE GOLDEN APPLES* (1949)

. . . . .

'Tis not love's going hurts my days,
But that it went in little ways.

EDNA ST. VINCENT MILLAY, *THE HARP-WEAVER* (1923)

. . . . .

Son, my son!
I will go up the mountain
and there I will light a fire
to the feet of my son's spirit,
and there I will lament him;
saying,
O my son,
what is my life to me, now you are departed?
Son, my son,
in the deep earth
we softly laid thee
in a chief's robe,
in a warrior's gear.
Surely there,
in the spirit land,
thy deeds attend thee!
Surely,
the corn comes to the ear again!
But I, here,
I am stalk that the seed-gatherers
descrying empty, afar, left standing.
Son, my son!
What is life to me, now you are departed?

PAIUTE INDIAN SONG, *LAMENT OF A MAN FOR HIS SON*

. . . . .

Sorrow was like the wind.
It came in gusts.

MARJORIE KINNAN RAWLINGS, *SOUTH MOON UNDER* (1933)

. . . . .

I cannot say what loves have come and gone;
I only know that summer sang in me
A little while, that in me sings no more.

EDNA ST. VINCENT MILLAY, *THE HARP-WEAVER* (1923)

.   .   .   .   .

From The Spring and the Fall I could not recall how much
time had passed
for somehow or other pain is timeless, absolute.
It has removed itself from space.
It always has been and always will be for it exists independent
of relations.
I feel it as myself, and when it ceases I will cease.

EVELYN SCOTT, *ESCAPADE* (1923)

.   .   .   .   .

What Lips My Lips Have Kissed, and Where, and Why
We do not die of anguish, we live on.
We continue to suffer.
We drink the cup drop by drop.

GEORGE SAND (1834), IN MARIE JENNY HOWE, ED., *THE INTIMATE JOURNAL OF
GEORGE SAND* (1929)

.   .   .   .   .

It was as if I had worked for years on the wrong side of a
tapestry,
learning accurately all its lines and figures,
yet always missing its color and sheen.

ANNA LOUISE STRONG, *I CHANGE WORLDS* (1935)

.   .   .   .   .

A man's sorrow runs uphill;
true it is difficult for him to bear,
but it is also difficult for him to keep.

DJUNA BARNES, *NIGHTWOOD* (1937)

.   .   .   .   .

There were many ways of breaking a heart. Stories were full of
hearts being broken by love, but what really broke a heart was
taking away its dream—whatever that dream might be.

PEARL BUCK, *THE PATRIOT* (1939)

.   .   .   .   .

The sun has set in your life; it is getting cold. The hundreds of
people around you cannot console you for the loss of the one.

MARIA AUGUSTA TRAPP, *THE STORY OF THE TRAPP FAMILY SINGERS* (1949)

.   .   .   .   .

The sorrows of humanity are no one's sorrows . . . .
A thousand people drowned in floods in China are news:
a solitary child drowned in a pond is a tragedy.

JOSEPHINE TEY, *THE DAUGHTER OF TIME* (1951)

.   .   .   .   .

Iron, left in the rain
And fog and dew with rust is covered. Pain
Rusts into beauty too.
I know full well that this is so:
I had a heartbreak long ago.

MARY CAROLYN DAVISE, RUST, FROM THE *HOME BOOK OF MODERN VERSE*
(1953)

.   .   .   .   .

Have you ever thought, when something dreadful happens, "A
moment ago things were not like this; let it be *then*, not *now*,
anything but *now*"? And you try and try to remake *then*, but
you know you can't. So you try to hold the moment quite still
and not let it move on and show itself.

MARY STEWART, *NINE COACHES WAITING* (1958)

.   .   .   .   .

The fire of pain traces for my soul
a luminous path across her sorrow.

RABINDRANATH TAGORE, *FIREFLIES* (1955)

.   .   .   .   .

Many people misjudge the permanent effect of sorrow,
and their capacity to live in the past.

IVY COMPTON-BURNETT, *MOTHER AND SON* (1955)

. . . . .

Where you used to be, there is a hole in the world, which I find myself constantly walking around in the daytime, and falling into at night. I miss you like hell.

EDNA ST. VINCENT MILLAY (1920), IN ALLAN ROSS MACDOUGALL, ED.,
LETTERS OF EDNA ST. VINCENT MILLAY (1952)

. . . . .

The human heart does not stay away too long from that which hurt it most. There is a return journey to anguish that few of us are released from making.

LILLIAN SMITH, THE JOURNEY (1954)

. . . . .

In the history of thought and culture the dark nights have perhaps
in some ways cost mankind less grief than the false dawns,
the prison houses in which hope persists [provides] less grief than the Promised Lands where hope expires.

LOUIS KRONENBERGER, COMPANY MATTERS (1954)

. . . . .

It's a kind of test, Mary, and it's the only kind that amounts to anything.
When something rotten like this happens,
then you have your choice.
You start to really be alive, or you start to die.
That's all.

JAMES AGEE, A DEATH IN THE FAMILY (1957)

. . . . .

So this was fame at last!
Nothing but a vast debt to be paid to the world in energy, blood, and time.

MAY SARTON, MRS. STEVENS HEARS THE MERMAIDS SINGING (1965)

. . . . .

No one comes near here
Morning or night. The desolate grasses
Grow out of sight.
Only the wild hare
Strays, then is gone.
The Landlord is silence
The tenant is dawn.

FRIEDA FROMM-REICHMANN, *LONELINESS* (1957)

. . . . .

It is hard to have patience with people who say, "There is no death" or "Death doesn't matter." There is death. And whatever is matters. And whatever happens has consequences, and it and they are irrevocable and irreversible. You might as well say birth doesn't matter. I look up at the night sky. Is there anything more certain that in all those vast times and spaces, if I were allowed to search them, I should nowhere find her face, her voice, her touch? She died. She is dead. Is the word so difficult to learn?

C. S. LEWIS, *A GRIEF OBSERVED* (1957)

. . . . .

Grief can't be shared.
Everyone carries it alone, his own burden, his own way.

ANNE MORROW LINDBERGH, *DEARLY BELOVED* (1962)

. . . . .

All that day I walked alone. In the afternoon I looked for a church, went into a cafe, and finally left on the bus, carrying with me more grief and sorrow than I had ever borne before, my body in tatters and my whole life a moan.

OSCAR LEWIS, *A DEATH IN THE SANCHEZ FAMILY* (1969)

. . . . .

The anxiety of meaninglessness
is anxiety about the loss of an ultimate concern,
of a meaning which gives meaning to all meanings.
This anxiety is aroused by the loss of a spiritual center,
of an answer, however symbolic and indirect,
to the question of the meaning of existence.

PAUL TILLICH, *THE COURAGE TO BE* (1973)

. . . . .

One must go through periods of numbness
that are harder to bear than grief.

ANNE MORROW LINDBERGH, *HOUR OF GOLD, HOUR OF LEAD* (1973)

. . . . .

Awareness is not something that we can achieve
and then go on to bigger and better things.

SARAH FERGUSON, *A GUARD WITHIN* (1974)

. . . . .

"Oh Mum! Oh Mum!"
There was what sounded like a gasp, or a sob.
"Mum, Dane's dead. Dane's dead!"
A pit opened at her feet. Down and down and down it went,
and had no bottom. Meggie slid into it, felt its lips close over
her head, and understood that she would never come out again
as long as she lived. What more could the gods do? She hadn't
known when she asked it.

COLLEEN MCCULLOUGH, *THE THORN BIRDS* (1977)

. . . . .

Every sorrow suggests a thousand songs, and every song recalls
a thousand sorrows, and so they are infinite in number, and all
the same.

MARILYNNE ROBINSON, *HOUSEKEEPING* (1980)

. . . . .

Lord, what I loved the most you tore from me.
Now hear again this heart cry out alone.
Your will was done, O Lord, against my own.
Lord, we're alone now, my heart and the sea.

ANTONIO MACHADO, *THE DREAM BELOW THE SUN* (1981)

. . . . .

There are other ways of knowing that are hindered by the light.

STEPHANIE KAZA, *THE ATTENTIVE HEART* (1993)

. . . . .

Three words were in the captain's heart. He shaped them
soundlessly with his trembling lips, as he had not breath to
spare for a whisper "I am lost." And having given up on life, the
captain suddenly began to live.

CARSON MCCULLERS, *REFLECTIONS IN A GOLDEN EYE* (1986)

. . . . .

Go with the pain, let it take you .... Open your palms and
your body to the pain. It comes in waves like a tide, and you
must be open as a vessel lying on the beach, letting it fill you up
and then, retreating, leaving you empty and clear .. With a
deep breath—it has to be as deep as the pain—one reaches a
kind of inner freedom from pain, as though the pain were not
yours but your body's. The spirit lays the body on the altar.

ANNE MORROW LINDBERGH, *WAR WITHIN AND WITHOUT* (1981)

. . . . .

Being lonely is a time of crucial significance, an entering into
an unknown search, mystery, a unique and special moment of
beauty, love, or joy, or a particular moment of pain, despair,
disillusionment, doubt, or rejection.

CLARK MOUSTAKAS, *LONELINESS AND LOVE* (1986)

. . . . .

Only that which is deeply felt can change us. Rational arguments alone cannot penetrate the layers of fear and conditioning that comprise our crippling belief system.

MARILYN FERGUSON, *THE AQUARIAN CONSPRIRACY* (1980)

. . . . .

One does not die from pain unless one chooses to.

WAKAKO YAMAUCHI, MAKAPUU BAY, IN *MAKING WAVES: AN ANTHOLOGY OF WRITINGS BY AND ABOUT ASIAN AMERICAN WOMEN* (1989)

. . . . .

There is nothing sadder than the cheerful letters of the dead, expressing hopes that were never fulfilled, ambitions that were never achieved, dreams cut off before they could come to fruition.

ELIZABETH PETERS, "SUFFERING BELONGS TO NO LANGUAGE," *NAKED ONCE MORE* (1989)

. . . . .

Sometimes pain was a crutch to hold on to when the only alternative was nothing at all.

SYLVIE SOMMERFIELD, *BITTERSWEET* (1991)

. . . . .

Between nothing and grief, I will take grief.

WILLIAM FAULKNER, *THE WILD PALMS* (1991)

. . . . .

True love and prayer are learned in the hour when love becomes impossible and the heart has turned to stone.

THOMAS MERTON, IN JACK KORNFIELD, *A PATH WITH HEART* (1993)

Discovering What Remains:
Healing, Solitude,
and Gaining Perspective

I_n this second phase of grief, the meaningful aspects of what remains are recognized and remembered. In remembering, we begin to heal, to acknowledge the essence of what is missing. It is a time to simply "be," to limit the "doings" that life demands.

This healing can be a time-consuming and exhausting process, often involving the rediscovery of the simple and the sensory. This can be a peaceful time, when obligations and responsibilities can be put aside. It is not usually an active time; it is time spent quietly, often in solitude, listening to soothing music and reading comforting poetry or books, taking time for a massage, going fishing, or enjoying a walk in the woods or a day at the beach.

Ultimately, healing helps us to gain perspective about loss and what it means, now and in the future. For this perspective to emerge, we need to be more objective and open, vulnerable yet strong. We need to ask if enough remains to risk living fully again. Is it worth the hurt and fear to date again after a partner's death? Can we make plans, knowing that disaster has struck in the past? Can we tolerate feeling disloyal if we turn to new possibilities and challenges and move away from our loss?

When we risk growing, ways are found to advance from the losses, to accept or to adjust to them, and to open to the possibility of grief transforming them into opportunities. Indeed, as many of the quotes in this section attest, it is the paradox of grief that we can continue to grow and love in spite of losing what we previously considered essential to life itself.

Healing and Solitude

. . . .

The Lord is my shepherd; I shall not want.
He maketh me to lie down in green pastures:
he leadeth me beside the still waters.
He restoreth my soul:
he leadeth me in the paths of righteousness for his name's sake.
Yea, though I walk through the valley of the shadow of death,
  I will fear no evil: for thou art with me;
  thy rod and thy staff they comfort me.
Thou preparest a table before me
  in the presence of mine enemies:
thou anointest my head with oil;
my cup runneth over.
Surely goodness and mercy shall follow me
  all the days of my life:
and I will dwell in the house of the Lord for ever.

PSALM 23

. . . .

Out of the depths have I cried unto thee, O Lord.
Lord, hear my voice.

PSALM 130:1-2

. . . .

No act of kindness, no matter how small, is ever wasted.

AESOP (FL. C. 550 B.C.), THE LION AND THE MOUSE

. . . . .

Blessed is he whose transgression is forgiven,
    whose sin is covered.
Blessed is the man unto whom the Lord imputeth not iniquity,
    and in whose spirit there is no guile.
When I kept silence, my bones waxed old through my roaring
all the day long.
For day and night thy hand was heavy upon me:
my moisture is turned into the drought of summer.
Selah.
I acknowledged my sin unto thee,
    and mine iniquity have I not hid.
I said, I will confess my transgressions unto the Lord;
    and thou forgavest the iniquity of my sin.
Selah.

PSALM 32:1-5

. . . . .

Two are better than one;
because they have a good reward for their labour.
For if they fall, the one will lift up his fellow:
but woe him that is alone when he falleth;
for he hath not another to help him up.

ECCLESIASTICS 4:9-10

. . . . .

Smiling through tears.

HOMER (C. 700 B.C.), *THE ILIAD*, BK. VI, L. 484

. . . . .

Prayer indeed is good,
but while calling on the gods
a man should himself lend a hand.

HIPPOCRATES, *REGIMEN*, BK.IV, SEC. 87,

. . . . .

A faithful friend is the medicine of life.

THE APOCRYPHA, THE WISDOM OF JESUS THE SON OF SIRACH, OR ECCLESIASTICUS, 6:16

. . . . .

✳ If someone comes to you asking for help, do not say in refusal,
"Trust in God. God will help you."
Rather, act as if there is no God,
and no one to help except you.

HASIDIC TEACHING

. . . . .

What soap is for the body,
tears are for the soul.

JEWISH PROVERB

. . . . .

May the Great Mystery
make sunrise in your heart.

SIOUX PRAYER

. . . . .

Honor a physician with the honor due unto him
for the uses which ye may have of him:
for the Lord hath created him.

THE APOCRYPHA, THE WISDOM OF JESUS THE SON OF SIRACH, OR ECCLESIASTICUS
38:1

. . . . .

For, lo, the wisdom is past, the rain is over and gone;
The flowers appear on the earth; the time of the singing of
birds is come, and the voice of the turtle is heard in our land;
The fig tree putteth forth her green figs
and the vines with the tender grape give a good smell.

SONG OF SOLOMON 2:11-13

.   .   .   .   .

Time eases all things.

> SOPHOCLES (C. 495-406 B.C.), *OEDIPUS REX*, L. 1515

.   .   .   .   .

Hope is a waking dream.

> ARISTOTLE (384-322 B.C.), IN DIOGENES LAERTIUS, *LIVES OF EMINENT PHILOSOPHERS*, BK. V, SEC. 18

.   .   .   .   .

While there's life, there's hope.

> TERENCE (C. 190-159 B.C.), *HEAUTON TIMOROUMENOS (THE SELF-TORMENTOR)*, L. 981

.   .   .   .   .

... be not afraid, neither be thou dismayed ....

> JOSHUA 1:9

.   .   .   .   .

And ye shall know the truth, and the truth shall make you free.

> JOHN 8:32

.   .   .   .   .

It is sweet to mingle tears with tears;
Griefs, where they wound in solitude,
Wound more deeply.

> SENECA, *LETTERS TO LUCILIUS* (80 A.D.)

.   .   .   .   .

There is something pleasureable in calm remembrance of a past sorrow.

> CICERO, *AD FAMILIARES* (40 B.C.)

.   .   .   .   .

A day is lost if one has not laughed

> FRENCH PROVERB

. . . . .

Beauty is before me, and
beauty behind me,
above me and below me
hovers the beautiful.
I am surrounded by it,
I am immersed in it.
In my youth, I am aware of it,
and, in old age,
I shall walk quietly the beautiful trail.
In beauty it is begun.
In beauty, it is ended.

NAVAHO SAYING

. . . . .

Deep peace of the running wave to you.
Deep peace of the flowing air to you.
Deep peace of the quiet earth to you.
Deep peace of the shining stars to you.
Deep peace of the infinite peace to you.

GAELIC RUNES

. . . . .

Bless to me, O God, the earth beneath my feet,
Bless to me, O God, the path whereon I go,
Bless to me, O God, the people whom I meet,
Today, tonight and tomorrow.

CELTIC BLESSING

. . . . .

He [Jesus] did not say, "You will never have a rough passage,
you will never be over-strained, you will never feel
uncomfortable,"
but he did say, "You will never be overcome."

JULIAN OF NORWICH, REVELATIONS OF DIVINE LOVE (1373)

. . . . .

A cheerful giver does not count the cost of what he gives.
His heart is set on pleasing and cheering him to whom the gift
is given.

JULIAN OF NORWICH, *REVELATIONS OF DIVINE LOVE* (1373)

. . . . .

Humankind is called to co-create.
With nature's help, humankind can set into creation
all that is necessary and life-sustaining.

HILDEGARDE VON BINGEN,(C. 1100) IN MATTHEW FOX, *ORIGINAL BLESSINGS*
(1983)

. . . . .

Nothing great was ever done without much enduring.

ST. CATHERINE OF SIENA (C. 1370), *ST. CATHERINE OF SIENA AS SEEN IN HER
LETTERS* (1911)

. . . . .

Patient endurance
Attaineth to all things.

SAINT TERESA OF AVILA, (C. 1550) IN JOANNA BANKIER AND DEIRDRE
LASHGARI, EDS., *WOMEN POETS OF THE WORLD* (1983)

. . . . .

The kiss you take is better than you give.

WILLIAM SHAKESPEARE, *TROILUS AND CRESSIDA* (1601-1602), ACT. IV, SC. V, L. 38

. . . . .

But if the while I think on thee, dear friend,
All losses are restor'd and sorrows end.

WILLIAM SHAKESPEARE, SONNET 30 (PUBLISHED 1609), L. 13

. . . . .

Give sorrow words; the grief that does not speak
Whispers the o'er-fraught heart and bids it break.

WILLIAM SHAKESPEARE, *MACBETH* (1606), ACT IV, SC. III, L. 209

. . . . .

To weep is to make less the depth of grief.

WILLIAM SHAKESPEARE, *KING HENRY THE SIXTH*, PART III (1590-1591), ACT II, SC. I, L. 85

. . . . .

Macbeth: Canst thou not minister to a mind diseas'd,
Pluck from the memory a rooted sorrow,
Raze out the written troubles of the brain,
And with some sweet oblivious antidote
Cleanse the stuff'd bosom of that perilous stuff
Which weighs upon the heart?
Doctor: Therein the patient
Must minister to himself.

WILLIAM SHAKESPEARE, *MACBETH* (1606), ACT V, SC. III, L. 40

. . . . .

Grief melts away
Like snow in May,
As if there were no such cold thing.

GEORGE HERBERT, "THE FLOWER," ST. 1, *THE TEMPLE* (1633)

. . . . .

By all means use some times to be alone.

GEORGE HERBERT, "THE CHURCH PORCH," ST. 25, *THE TEMPLE* (1633)

. . . . .

Who would have thought my shrivel'd heart
Could have recover'd greenness?

GEORGE HERBERT, "THE FLOWER," ST. 2, *THE TEMPLE* (1633)

. . . . .

By speaking of our misfortunes we often relieve them.

PIERRE CORNEILLE, POLYEUCTE (1640), ACT I, SC. 3

. . . . .

On the wings of Time grief flies away.

JEAN DE LA FONTAINE, *FABLES*, BK. VI (1668), FABLE 21

. . . . .

And now in age I bud again,
After so many deaths I live and write;
I once more smell the dew and rain,
And relish versing: O my only light,
It cannot be
That I am he
On whom thy tempests fell all night.

GEORGE HERBERT, "THE FLOWER," ST. 6, *THE TEMPLE* (1633)

. . . . .

We must laugh before we are happy,
for fear we die before we laugh at all.

JEAN DE LA BRUYÈRE, *LES CARACTÈRES* (1688). DU COEUR

. . . . .

None know the weight of another's burthen.

GEORGE HERBERT, *JACULA PRUDENTUM* (1651), NO. 880

. . . . .

It is always darkest just before the day dawneth.

THOMAS FULLER, *PISGAH SIGHT* (1650), BK. II, CH. 2

. . . . .

For solitude sometimes is best society,
And short retirement urges sweet return.

JOHN MILTON, *PARADISE LOST* (1667) BK. IX, L. 249

. . . . .

Rich tears! What power lies in those falling drops.

MARY DELARIVIERE MANLEY, *THE ROYAL MISCHIEF* (1696)

. . . . .

Amazing grace! how sweet the sound,
That saved a wretch like me!
I once was lost, but now am found,
Was blind, but now I see.

JOHN NEWTON (1725-1807), "AMAZING GRACE"

. . . . .

Hope, like the gleaming taper's light,
Adorns and cheers our way;
And still, as darker grows the night,
Emits a brighter ray.

OLIVER GOLDSMITH, THE CAPTIVITY, AN ORATORIO (1764), ACT II

. . . . .

Can I see another's woe,
And not be in sorrow too?
Can I see another's grief,
And not seek for kind relief?

WILLIAM BLAKE, "ON ANOTHER'S SORROW," ST. 1, SONGS OF INNOCENCE (1789)

. . . . .

The music in my heart I bore
Long after it was heard no more.

WILLIAM WORDSWORTH, THE SOLITARY REAPER (1807), ST. 4

. . . . .

Soldier, rest! thy warfare o'er,
Sleep the sleep that knows not breaking,
Dream of battled fields no more,
Days of danger, nights of waking.

SIR WALTER SCOTT, THE LADY OF THE LAKE (1810), CANTO I, ST. 31

. . . . .

Even when the affections are not strongly moved by any
superior excellence, the companions of our childhood always
possess a certain power over our minds which hardly any later
friend can obtain.

MARY SHELLEY, FRANKENSTEIN (1818)

. . . . .

We are rich only through what we give,
and poor only through what we refuse.

ANNE-SOPHIE SWETCHINE, IN COUNT DE FALLOUX, ED., THE WRITINGS OF
MADAME SWETCHINE (1869)

. . . . .

I never found the companion that was so companionable as solitude.

HENRY DAVID THOREAU, *WALDEN* (1854)

. . . . .

The delicate and infirm go for sympathy, not to the well and buoyant, but to those who have suffered like themselves.

CATHARINE ESTHER BEECHER, *WOMAN SUFFRAGE AND WOMAN'S PROFESSIONS* (1871)

. . . . .

We want people to feel with us more than to act for us.

GEORGE ELIOT (1856), IN J. W. CROSS, ED., *GEORGE ELIOT'S LIFE AS RELATED IN HER LETTERS AND JOURNALS* (1884)

. . . . .

He who is sorrowful can force himself to smile, but he who is glad cannot weep.

SELMA LAGERLOF, *THE STORY OF GOSTA BERLING* (1891)

. . . . .

Those whom we support hold us up in life.

MARIE VON EBNER-ESCHENBACH, *APHORISMS* (1893)

. . . . .

Yes'm, old friends is always best, 'less you can catch a new one that's fit to make an old one out of.

SARAH ORNE JEWETT, *THE COUNTRY OF THE POINTED FIRS* (1896)

. . . . .

Grief tires more than anything,
and brings a deeper slumber.

GEORGE LOUIS PALMELLA BUSSON DU MAURIER, *TRILBY* (1894), PART VIII

．　．　．　．　．

That life is worth living is the most necessary of assumptions, and, were it not assumed, the most impossible of conclusions.

GEORGE SANTAYANA, THE LIFE OF REASON (1905-1906), VOL. 1

．　．　．　．　．

All sorrows can be borne if you put them into a story or tell a story about them.

ISAK DINESEN

．　．　．　．　．

When we can begin to take our failures non-seriously, it means we are ceasing to be afraid of them. It is of immense importance to learn to laugh at ourselves.

KATHERINE MANSFIELD (1922), JOURNAL OF KATHERINE MANSFIELD (1927)

．　．　．　．　．

Only solitary men know the full joys of friendship. Others have their family; but to a solitary and an exile his friends are everything.

WILLA CATHER, SHADOWS ON THE ROCK (1931)

．　．　．　．　．

Fond as we are of our loved ones, there comes at times during their absence an unexplained peace.

ANNE SHAW, BUT SUCH IS LIFE (1931)

．　．　．　．　．

Nobody on the outside, no not even God Himself, knows what a man suffers on the inside. There's no language to convey it. It's beyond all human comprehension. It's so vast, so wide, so deep that even the angels with all their powers of understanding and all their powers of locomotion could never explore the whole of it. Now when a friend makes a call on you you've got to obey. You have to do for him what God Himself wouldn't do. It's the law. Otherwise you'd fall apart, you'd bark in the night like a dog.

HENRY MILLER, THE AIR CONDITIONED NIGHTMARE (1970)

. . . . .

Folks differs, dearie. They differs a lot. Some can stand things
that others can't. There's never no way of knowin' how much
they can stand.

ANN PETRY, *THE STREET* (1946)

. . . . .

The storm of the last night has crowned his morning with
golden peace.

RABINDRANATH TAGORE, *STRAY BIRDS* (1945)

. . . . .

Blessed are those who can give without remembering,
and take without forgetting.

ELIZABETH BIBESCO, IN JACOB BRAUDE, *SECOND ENCYCLOPEDIA OF STORIES,
QUOTATIONS, AND ANECDOTES* (1957)

. . . . .

Each friend represents a world in us, a world possibly not born
until they arrive, and it is only by this meeting that a new
world is born.

ANAIS NIN (1937), *THE DIARY OF ANAIS NIN*, VOL. 2 (1967)

. . . . .

My feeling is that there is nothing in life but refraining from
hurting others, and comforting those that are sad.

OLIVE SHREINER, *THE LETTERS OF OLIVE SHREINER* (1976)

. . . . .

We were surprised and disappointed that people we thought
were good friends became distant, uneasy and seemed unable
to help us. Others who were casual acquaintances became
suddenly close, sustainers of life for us. Grief changes the rules,
and sometimes rearranges the combinations.

MARTHA WHITMORE HICKMAN, *HEALING AFTER LOSS* (1994)

Gaining Perspective

.   .   .   .   .

Sorrow <u>is</u> better than laughter: for by the sadness of the
countenance the heart is made better.

ECCLESIASTES 7:3

.   .   .   .   .

. . . naked came I out of my mother's womb, and naked shall I
return thither: the Lord gave, and the Lord hath taken away;
blessed be the name of the Lord.

JOB 1:21

.   .   .   .   .

Give me neither poverty nor riches.

PROVERBS 30:8

.   .   .   .   .

Rejoice not over thy greatest enemy being dead,
but remember that we die all.

THE APOCRYPHA, THE WISDOM OF JESUS THE SON OF SIRACH, OR ECCLESIASTICUS, 8:7

.   .   .   .   .

Forsake not an old friend; for the new is not comparable to
him:
a new friend is as new wine;
when it is old, thou shalt drink it with pleasure.

THE APOCRYPHA, THE WISDOM OF JESUS THE SON OF SIRACH, OR ECCLESIASTICUS 9:10

.   .   .   .   .

He that is today a king
tomorrow shall die.

THE APOCRYPHA, *THE WISDOM OF JESUS THE SON OF SIRACH*, OR *ECCLESIASTICUS* 10:10

.   .   .   .   .

A friend cannot be known in prosperity:
and an enemy cannot be hidden in adversity.

THE APOCRYPHA, *THE WISDOM OF JESUS THE SON OF SIRACH*, OR *ECCLESIASTICUS* 12:8

.   .   .   .   .

Someone, I tell you
will remember us.
We are oppressed by
fears of oblivion.

SAPPHO (C. 612 B.C.) *SOMEONE, I TELL YOU*

.   .   .   .   .

Death is an ill; 'tis thus the Gods decide:
For had death been a boon, the Gods had died.

SAPPHO (C. 612 B.C.) IN C. R. HAINES, ED., *SAPPHO: THE POEMS AND FRAGMENTS* (1926)

.   .   .   .   .

Nothing endures but change.

HERACLITUS (C. 540-C. 480 B.C.), IN DIOGENES LAERTIUS, *LIVES OF EMINENT PHILOSOPHERS*, BK IX, SEC. 8, AND PLATO, *CRATYLUS*, 402A

.   .   .   .   .

Much learning does not teach understanding.

HERACLITUS (C. 540-C. 480 B.C.), *ON THE UNIVERSE*, FRAGMENT 16

.   .   .   .   .

The greatest griefs are those we cause ourselves.

SOPHOCLES (C. 495-406 B.C.), *OEDIPUS REX*, L. 1230

. . . . .

Comfort ye, comfort ye my people, saith your God.
Speak ye comfortably to Jerusalem, and cry unto her,
that her warfare is accomplished, that her iniquity is pardoned:
for she hath received of the Lord's hand double for all her sins.
The voice of him that crieth in the wilderness,
Prepare ye the way of the Lord, make straight in the desert
    a highway for our God.
Every valley shall be exalted, and every mountain
    and hill shall be made low:
and the crooked shall be made straight,
    and the rough places plain:
And the glory of the Lord shall be revealed,
    and all flesh shall see it together:
    for the mouth of the Lord hath spoken it.
The voice said, Cry. And he said, What shall I cry?
All flesh is grass, and all the goodliness thereof is
    as the flower of the field:
The grass withereth, the flower fadeth:
    because the spirit of the Lord bloweth upon it:
    surely the people is grass. The grass withereth,
    the flower fadeth:
    but the word of our God shall stand for ever.

    ISAIAH 40:1-8

. . . . .

He who learns must suffer.
And even in our sleep
pain that cannot forget falls drop by drop upon the heart,
and in our own despair, against our will,
comes wisdom to us by the awful grace of God.

    AESCHYLUS (525-456 B.C.), AGAMEMNON, L. 177

. . . . .

Misfortune shows those who are not really friends.

    ARISTOTLE (384-322 B.C.), EUDEMIAN ETHICS, BK. VII, CH. 2

. . . . .

Circumstances rule men;
men do not rule circumstances.

HERODOTUS (C. 485-425 B.C.), *THE HISTORIES OF HERODOTUS*, BK.VII, CH. 49

. . . . .

Things which you do not hope happen more frequently than
things which you do hope.

TITUS MACCIUS PLAUTUS (254-184 B.C.), *MOSTELLARIA*, ACT I, SC. III, L. 40

. . . . .

For what is a man profited,
if he shall gain the whole world,
and lose his own soul?

MATTHEW 16:26

. . . . .

The scars of others should teach us caution.

SAINT JEROME (C. 342-420), *LETTER 54*

. . . . .

An ill wind that bloweth no man to good.

JOHN HEYWOOD, *PROVERBS* (1546), PT. II, CH. 9

. . . . .

Shared joy is double joy
and shared sorrow is half sorrow.

SWEDISH PROVERB

. . . . .

Though it be honest, it is never good
To bring bad news.

WILLIAM SHAKESPEARE, *ANTONY AND CLEOPATRA* (1606-1607), ACT II, SC. V, L. 85

. . . . .

We need greater virtues to sustain good fortune than bad.

FRANÇOIS, DUC DE LA ROCHEFOUCAULD, "MAXIM 25," *REFLECTIONS; OR,
SENTENCES AND MORAL MAXIMS* (1678)

. . . . .

If we had no winter, the spring would not be so pleasant:
if we did not sometimes taste of adversity,
prosperity would not be so welcome.

Anne Bradstreet (c. 1612-1672), *Thirty-three Meditations*, 14

. . . . .

When to the sessions of sweet silent thought
I summon up remembrance of things past,
I sigh the lack of many a thing I sought,
And with old woes new wail my dear times' waste.

William Shakespeare, *Sonnet 30* (published 1609), l. 1

. . . . .

We are never so happy nor so unhappy as we imagine.

François, Duc de La Rochefoucauld, "Maxim 49," *Reflections; or,
Sentences and Moral Maxims* (1678),

. . . . .

Nothing exists from whose nature some effect does not follow.

Benedict (Baruch) Spinoza, *Ethics* (1677), pt. I, proposition 36

. . . . .

The joy of life is variety; the tenderest love requires to be
renewed by intervals of absense.

Samuel Johnson, *The Idler* (1758-1760), no. 39

. . . . .

Naked were we born and naked must we depart . . . .
No matter what you may lose,
be patient for nothing belongs;
it is only lent.

Gluckel of Hameln, *Memories of Gluckel of Hameln* (1724)

. . . . .

Joys impregnate:
Sorrows bring forth.

WILLIAM BLAKE, PROVERBS OF HELL (1790)

. . . . .

A talent is formed in stillness, a character in the world's
torrent.

JOHANN WOLFGANG VON GOETHE, *TORQUATO TASSO* (1790), ACT I, SC. II

. . . . .

There is strong shadow where there is much light.

JOHANN WOLFGANG VON GOETHE, *GÄTZ VON BERLICHINGEN* (1773), ACT I

. . . . .

Who ne'er his bread in sorrow ate,
Who ne'er the mournful midnight hours
Weeping upon his bed has sate,
He knows you not, ye Heavenly Powers.

JOHANN WOLFGANG VON GOETHE, *WILHELM MEISTER'S APPRENTICESHIP* (1786-
1830), BK. II, CH. 13

. . . . .

It takes two to speak the truth—one to speak, and another
to hear.

HENRY DAVID THOREAU, "WEDNESDAY," *A WEEK ON THE CONCORD AND
MERRIMACK RIVERS* (1849)

. . . . .

Nothing except a battle lost can be half so melancholy as a
battle won.

ARTHUR WELLESLEY, DUKE OF WELLINGTON, *DISPATCH FROM THE FIELD OF
WATERLOO* (JUNE 1815)

. . . . .

It is better to drink of deep griefs
than to taste shallow pleasures.

WILLIAM HAZLITT, *CHARACTERISTICS* (1823)

. . . . .

Into each life some rain must fall,
Some days must be dark and dreary.

HENRY WADSWORTH LONGFELLOW, *THE RAINY DAY* (1842), ST. 3

. . . . .

The boundaries which divide Life
from Death are at best shadowy and vague.
Who shall say where the one ends,
and where the other begins?

EDGAR ALLEN POE, *THE PREMATURE BURIAL* (1844)

. . . . .

Great joys weep,
great sorrows laugh.

JOSEPH ROUX, *MEDITATIONS OF A PARISH PRIEST* (1886)

. . . . .

Experience is the comb
that nature gives us
when we are bald.

BELGIAN PROVERB

. . . . .

Every sweet has its sour;
every evil its good.

RALPH WALDO EMERSON, "COMPENSATION," *ESSAYS: FIRST SERIES* (1841).

. . . . .

For everything you have missed, you have gained something
else; and for everything you gain, you lose something.

RALPH WALDO EMERSON, "COMPENSATION," *ESSAYS: FIRST SERIES* (1841).

. . . . .

Great grief is a divine and terrible radiance
which transfigures the wretched.

VICTOR HUGO, *LES MISERABLES* (1862), FANTINE, BK. V, CH. 13

. . . . .

Grief may be joy misunderstood;
Only the Good discerns the good.

ELIZABETH BARRETT BROWNING, *DE PROFUNDIS* (1862), ST. 21

. . . . .

The youth gets together his
materials to build a bridge to the moon, or,
perchance, a palace or temple on the earth,
and, at length, the middle-aged man
concludes to build a woodshed with them.

HENRY DAVID THOREAU, "JULY 14, 1852," *JOURNAL* (1906).

. . . . .

Mishaps are like knives,
that either serve us or cut us,
as we grasp them by the blade or the handle.

JAMES RUSSELL LOWELL, "CAMBRIDGE THIRTY YEARS AGO," *LITERARY ESSAYS,*
VOL. I (1864-1890),

. . . . .

If we could read the secret history of our enemies we should
find in each man's life sorrow and suffering enough to disarm
all hostility.

HENRY WADSWORTH LONGFELLOW, *DRIFTWOOD* (1857)

. . . . .

Autumn to winter, winter into spring,
Spring into summer, summer into fall
So rolls the changing year, and so we change;
Motion so swift, we know not that we move.

DINAH MARIA MULOCK CRAIK, "IMMUTABLE," *MULOCK'S POEMS, NEW AND OLD* (1880).

. . . . .

People have to learn sometimes not only how much the heart,
but how much the head, can bear.

MARIA MITCHELL (1855), IN PHEBE MITCHELL KENDALL, ED., *MARIA
MITCHELL, LIFE, LETTERS, AND JOURNALS* (1896)

. . . . .

It was the best of times, it was the worst of times, it was the age of wisdom, it was the age of foolishness, it was the epoch of belief, it was the epoch of incredulity, it was the season of Light, it was the season of Darkness, it was the spring of hope, it was the winter of despair, we had everything before us, we had nothing before us, we were all going direct to Heaven, we were all going direct the other way—in short, the period was so far like the present period, that some of its noisiest authorities insisted on its being received, for good or for evil, in the superlative degree of comparison only.

CHARLES DICKENS, *A TALE OF TWO CITIES* (1848)

. . . . .

Time is
Too slow for those who Wait,
Too swift for those who Fear,
Too long for those who Grieve,
Too short for those who Rejoice,
But for those who Love
Time is not.

SAYING ON A SUNDIAL IN SARATOGA SPRINGS, NEW YORK

. . . . .

He had seen old views and patients
disappearing, one by one,
He had learned that Death is master
both of Science and Art.

WILL CARLETON, *THE COUNTRY DOCTOR* (1900)

. . . . .

Although the world is very full of suffering, it is full also of the overcoming of it.

HELEN KELLER, *OPTIMISM* (1903)

. . . . .

Everyone who is born holds dual citizenship, in the kingdom of the well and in the kingdom of the sick. Although we all prefer to use only the good passport, sooner or later each of us is obliged, at least for a spell, to indentify ourselves as citizens of that other place.

SUSAN SONTAG, *ILLNESS AS METAPHOR* (1978)

. . . . .

It's odd that you can get so anesthetized by your own pain or your own problem that you don't quite fully share the hell of someone close to you.

LADY BIRD JOHNSON, *A WHITE HOUSE DIARY* (1970)

. . . . .

Since every death diminishes us a little, we grieve not so much for the death as for ourselves.

LYNN CAINE, *WIDOW* (1974)

. . . . .

The truth that many people never understand until it is too late is that the more you try to avoid suffering the more you suffer.

THOMAS MERTON, *LOVE AND LIVING* (1979)

. . . . .

Snow was general all over Ireland. It was falling on every part of the dark central plain, on the treeless hills, falling softly upon the Bog of Allen and, farther westward, softly falling into the dark mutinous Shannon waves. It was falling, too, upon every part of the lonely churchyard on the hill where Michael Furey lay buried. It lay thickly drifted on the crooked crosses and headstones, on the spears of the little gate, on the barren thorns. His soul swooned slowly as he heard the snow falling faintly through the universe and faintly falling, like the descent of their last end, upon all the living and the dead.

JAMES JOYCE, "THE DEAD," *DUBLINERS* (1916).

. . . . .

Some memories are realities, and are better than anything that can ever happen to one again.

WILLA CATHER, *My Ántonia* (1918)

. . . . .

So many persons think divorce a panacea for every ill, who find out, when they try it, that the remedy is worse than the disease.

DOROTHY DIX, *Her Book* (1926)

. . . . .

I love my past. I love my present. I'm not ashamed of what I've had, and I'm not sad because I have it no longer.

COLETTE, *The Last of Cheri* (1926)

. . . . .

There is a land of the living and a land of the dead and the bridge is love, the only survival, the only meaning.

THORTON WILDER, *The Bridge of San Luis Rey* (1927)

. . . . .

Everything in life that we really accept undergoes a change.

KATHERINE MANSFIELD (1920), *Journal of Katherine Mansfield* (1927)

. . . . .

Everywhere I go, I find a poet has been there before me.

SIGMUND FREUD

. . . . .

It takes time for the absent to assume their true shape in our thoughts.

COLETTE, *Sido* (1930)

. . . . .

Sorrow is tranquility remembered in emotion.

DOROTHY PARKER, "Sentiment," *The Collected Stories of Dorothy Parker* (1942).

.   .   .   .   .

So much do I love wandering,
So much I love the sea and sky,
That it will be a piteous thing
In one small grave to lie.

ZOË AKINS, *THE WANDERER* (1937)

.   .   .   .   .

Sorrow makes us very good or very bad.

GEORGE SAND (1871), FROM *FRENCH WIT AND WISDOM* (1950)

.   .   .   .   .

It is better to learn early of the inevitable depths, for then
sorrow and death take their proper place in life, and one is not
afraid.

PEARL BUCK, *MY SEVERAL WORLDS* (1954)

.   .   .   .   .

... the loss of illusions and the discovery of identity, though
painful at first, can be ultimately exhilarating and
strengthening.

ABRAHAM MASLOW, *TOWARD A PSYCHOLOGY OF BEING* (1958)

.   .   .   .   .

Forgiving presupposes remembering.

PAUL TILLICH, *THE ETERNAL NOW* (1963)

.   .   .   .   .

However often marriage is dissolved, it remains indissoluble.
Real divorce, the divorce of heart and nerve and fiber, does not
exist, since there is no divorce from memory.

VIRGILIA PETERSON, *A MATTER OF LIFE AND DEATH* (1961)

.   .   .   .   .

In a total work, the failures have their not unimportant place.

MAY SARTON, *MRS. STEVENS HEARS THE MERMAIDS SINGING* (1965)

. . . . .

Our language has wisely sensed the two sides of being alone. It has created the word "loneliness" to express the pain of being alone. And it has created the word "solitude" to express the glory of being alone.

PAUL TILLICH, *THE ETERNAL NOW* (1963)

. . . . .

I do not believe that true optimism can come about except through tragedy.

MADELEINE L'ENGLE, *TWO-PART INVENTION* (1968)

. . . . .

It's exhilarating to be alive in a time of awakening consciousness; it can also be confusing, disorienting, and painful.

ADRIENNE RICH, "WHEN WE DEAD AWAKE: WRITING AS RE-VISION," *ON LIES, SECRETS, AND SILENCE* (1978).

. . . . .

Change is the constant, the signal for rebirth, the egg of the phoenix.

CHISTINA BALDWIN, *ONE TO ONE* (1977)

. . . . .

Success is a public affair. Failure is a private funeral.

ROSALIND RUSSELL, IN JOHN ROBERT COLOMBO, *POPCORN IN PARADISE* (1979)

. . . . .

I have never been anywhere but sick. In a sense sickness is a place, more instructive than a long trip to Europe, and it's always a place where there's no company, where nobody can follow. Sickness before death is a very appropriate thing and I think those who don't have it miss one of God's mercies.

FLANNERY O'CONNOR, IN SALLY FITZGERALD, ED., *THE HABIT OF BEING* (1979)

. . . . .

Birds sing after a storm; why shouldn't people feel as free to delight in whatever sunlight remains to them?

ROSE KENNEDY, *TIMES TO REMEMBER* (1974)

. . . . .

It's a good thing to have all the props pulled out from under us occasionally. It gives us some sense of what is rock under our feet, and what is sand.

MADELEINE L'ENGLE, *THE SUMMER OF THE GREAT-GRANDMOTHER* (1974)

. . . . .

That's the way the system works. Sometimes you get the bear, sometimes the bear gets you.

SUE GRAFTON, *"H" IS FOR HOMICIDE* (1991)

. . . . .

It seems inevitable now, looking back, that all of that could have been jumbled together the way it was. I am amazed that any of us survived it. But I guess the human race has survived worse. I know it has. The question is, at what cost? Because wounds do leave scars and scar tissue has no feeling. That's what people forget when they train their sons to be "men" by injuring them. There is a price for survival.

MARILYN FRENCH, *THE WOMEN'S ROOM* (1977)

. . . . .

Death in its way comes just as much of a surprise as birth.

EDNA O'BRIEN, *A ROSE IN THE HEART* (1978)

. . . . .

There is something disorderly about the death of a young person. In a universe disturbed by so much over which we have no control, an untimely tragedy rattles the teeth of our already shaken confidence. We want to domesticate death, fight it on our own turf, in familiar rooms with shades drawn evenly, top sheets turned back, and a circle of hushed voices closing in.

FAYE MOSKOWITZ, *A LEAK IN THE HEART* (1985)

. . . . .

Most successful people are unhappy. That's why they are successes—they have to reassure themselves about themselves by achieving something that the world will notice . . . The happy people are failures because they are on such good terms with themselves that they don't give a damn.

AGATHA CHRISTIE

. . . . .

Every now and then, life takes us in a big leap forward, sometimes, it seems, by the scruff of our necks.

MOLLY YOUNG BROWN, GROWING WHOLE (1993)

. . . . .

Divorce is the psychological equivalent of a triple coronary by-pass. After such a monumental assault on the heart, it can take a whole decade to amend all the habits and attitudes that led up to it.

MARY KAY BLAKELY, AMERICAN MOM (1994)

. . . . .

The worst thing about grief is the length of time during which the experience lasts. For the first weeks one is in a state of shock. But the agony lasts long after the state of shock comes to an end. After a year, or about two, the agony gives way to a dull ache, a sort of void. During the night in one's dreams, and in the morning when one wakes, one is vaguely aware that something is wrong and, when waking is complete, one knows exactly what it is.

LORD HAILSHAM OF ST. MARYLEBONE, A SPARROW'S FLIGHT (1991)

. . . . .

Success can eliminate as many options as failure.

TOM ROBBINS, EVEN COWGIRLS GET THE BLUES (1996)

Discovering What's Possible:
Integration, Re-thimking, and Transformation

The worst has passed and time has brought acceptance of the full reality of a loss. In this third phase of grief, it's time to find out what can be done with what we have left. There is a reason for survival, for keeping on in spite of everything. We finally are able to act "in sync" with ourselves and our values, either altering long-standing beliefs and myths or reaffirming them.

Having accepted the reality of loss and the limits of what is left, we take on tasks that include the rediscovery of life's potentials. But to do this we must integrate our losses into new life patterns, become self-empowered by rethinking what these losses mean, and ultimately transform losses to live full lives.

As the quotes in this section indicate, when we do this, a sense of wholeness and integrity emerges. No longer seeing through the same eyes, we affirm how deeply we are related to others. Nothing can take away the substance of who we are, what we're about, or the love that links us to others, living and dead, present or missing. We exceed the separateness of detachment and the finiteness of death.

I consider this section to be the richest, most creative, and most demanding of all the aspects of grieving. Those looking for the courage to move forward with their lives will find it here.

And yes, this is much easier said than done. But it does help to consider who is saying it!

Integration

Everything that has a beginning has an ending.
Make your peace with that and all will be well.

BUDDHA

Do not plan for ventures before finishing what's at hand.

EURIPEDES

You can't prevent birds of sorrow flying over your head—
but you can prevent them from building nests in your hair.

CHINESE PROVERB

The one who removes a mountain
Begins by carrying away small stones.

CHINESE PROVERB

It is better to go to the house of mourning,
than to go to the house of feasting.

ECCLESIASTES 7:2

Keep on sowing your seed,
for you never know which will grow—
perhaps it all will.

ECCLESIASTICS 11:6

. . . . .

Give not thy heart unto unending sorrow;
put it away, remembering the last end;
forget it not, for there is no returning again;
him thou shall not profit,
and thou will hurt thyself.
Remember, for him it was yesterday, and today is for thee.

ECCLESISTICUS 38:17

. . . . .

A journey of a thousand miles must begin with a single step.

LAO-TZU, *THE WAY OF LAO-TZU*, 64

. . . . .

Learning without thought is labor lost;
thought without learning is perilous.

CONFUCIUS, *THE CONFUCIAN ANALECTS*, 2:15

. . . . .

Endure, my heart: you once endured something even more
dreadful.

HOMER, *ODYSSEY*, BOOK XIX, LINE 18

. . . . .

Vengeance in mine;
I will repay, saith the Lord.

ROMANS 12:19

. . . . .

Death is better, a milder fate than tyranny.

THEMISTOCLES, *AGAMEMNON*, L. 1364

. . . . .

Waste not fresh tears over old griefs.

EURIPIDES, *ALEXANDER*, FRAGMENT 44

. . . . .

Life is short, the art long, opportunity fleeting, experiment
treacherous, judgement difficult.

HIPPOCRATES, *APHORISMS*, SEC. I, 1

. . . . .

Do not act as if you had ten thousand years to throw away.
Death stands at your elbow. Be good for something, while you
live and it is within your power.

MARCUS AURELIUS

. . . . .

The hour of departure has arrived, and we go our ways—
I to die, and you to live.
Which is better God only knows.

PLATO, *DIALOGUE*, APOLOGY, 42

. . . . .

Then Peter came to Jesus and asked:
"Lord if my brother keeps on sinning against me, how many
times do I have to forgive him? Seven times?"
"No, not seven times," answered Jesus,
"but seventy times seven."

MATTHEW 18:21-22

. . . . .

He that is without sin among you, let him first cast a stone at her.

JOHN 8:7

. . . . .

So when you are offering your gift at the altar,
if you remember that your brother or sister has something
against you,
leave your gift there before the altar
and go, first be reconciled to your brother or sister
and then come and offer your gift.

MATTHEW 5:23-24

. . . . .

Father, forgive them; for they know not what they do.

LUKE 23:34 (JESUS ON THE CROSS)

. . . . .

Grandfather,
Look at our brokeness.

We know that in all creation
Only the human family
Has strayed from the Sacred Way.

We know that we are the ones
Who are divided,

And we are the ones
Who must come back together
To walk in the Sacred Way.

Grandfather,
Sacred One,
Teach us love, compassion, and honor

That we may heal the earth
And heal each other.

FROM THE OJIBWAY INDIANS OF NORTH AMERICA

. . . . .

Can any of you by worrying add a single hour to
     the span of your life?
You know how to interpret the appearance of earth and sky,
but why do you not know how to interpret the present time?
Why do you see the speck in your neighbor's eye,
but do not notice the log in your own eye?
What does it profit them if they gain the whole world,
but lose or forfeit themselves?

LUKE

. . . . .

Be at peace with your own soul. Enter eagerly into the treasure house that is inside you. The ladder leading to the Kingdom is hidden within your soul. Dive into yourself, and in your soul you will discover the stairs by which to ascend.

ISAAC OF NINEVAH

. . . . .

Now let the weeping cease
Let no one mourn again
The love of God will bring you peace
There is no end.

THE GOSPEL AT COLONUS

. . . . .

Do you know that disease and death must overtake us, no matter what we are doing? What do you wish to be doing when it overtakes you? If you have anything better to be doing when you are so overtaken, get to work on that.

EPICTETUS

. . . . .

A good death does honor to a whole life.

PETRARCH (FRANCESCO PETRARCA) 1304-1374, TO LAURA IN DEATH, CANZONE 16

. . . . .

If I knew the world were coming to an end tomorrow, I would still go out and plant my three apple trees today.

MARTIN LUTHER

. . . . .

We pardon to the extent that we love.

FRANÇOIS, DUC DE LA ROCHEFOUCAULD, REFLECTIONS; OR, SENTENCES AND MORAL MAXIMS, (1678), MAXIM 330

. . . . .

The executioner is, I hear, very expert; and my neck is very slender.

ANNE BOLEYN (1536), IN WILLIS JOHN ABBOT, *NOTABLE WOMEN IN HISTORY* (1913)

. . . . .

Virtue is bold, and goodness never fearful.

WILLIAM SHAKESPEARE, *MEASURE FOR MEASURE*, ACT III, SC. I, L. 214

. . . . .

The road to resoution lies by doubt:
The next way home's the farthest way about.

FRANCIS QUARLES, *EMBLEMS* (1635) BK. IV, NO. 2, EPIGRAM

. . . . .

Words that weep and tears that speak.

ABRAHAM COWLEY, *THE PROPHET*

. . . . .

No longer mourn for me when I am dead
That you shall hear the surly sullen bell
Give warning to the world that I am fled
From this vile world, with vilest worms to dwell:
Nay, if you read this line, remember not
The hand that writ it; for I love you so
That I in your sweet thoughts would be forgot
If thinking on me should make you woe.
O, if, I say, you look upon this verse
When I perhaps compounded am with clay,
Do not so much as my poor name rehearse,
But let your love even with my life decay,
Lest the wise world should look into your moan
And mock you with me after I am gone.

WILLIAM SHAKESPEARE, *SONNETT LXXI*

. . . . .

O! now, forever,
Farewell the tranquil mind; farewell content!
Farewell the plumed troop and the big wars
That make ambition virtue! O, farewell!
Farewell the neighing steed, and the shrill trump,
The spririt-stirring drum, the ear-piercing fife,
The royal banner, and all quality,
Pride, pomp, and circumstance of glorious war!
And, O you mortal engines, whose rude throats
The immortal Jove's dread clamors counterfeit,
Farewell! Othello's occupation's gone!

WILLIAM SHAKESPEARE, *OTHELLO*, ACT III, SC. III, L. 348

. . . . .

It is a very melancholy reflection that men are usually so weak
that it is absolutely necessary for them to know sorrow and
pain to be in their right senses.

RICHARD STEELE, *THE SPECTATOR* (1711)

. . . . .

I am at the point of death.
I have finished before I could enjoy my talents.
Yet life is so beautiful, my career opened so auspiciously—
but fate is not to be changed . . . .
I thus finish my funeral song—I must not leave it
unaccomplished.

WOLFGANG AMADEUS MOZART AT AGE 36

. . . . .

You can be pleased with nothing when you are not pleased
with yourself.

LADY MARY WORTLEY MONTAGU, LETTER TO HER FUTURE HUSBAND (1712), IN
OCTAVE THANET, ED., *THE BEST LETTERS OF LADY MARY WORTLEY MONTAGU*
(1901)

. . . . .

If you trap the moment before it's ripe,
The tears of repentence you'll certainly wipe;
But if once you let the ripe moment go
You can never wipe off the tears of woe.

WILLIAM BLAKE, "IF YOU TRAP THE MOMENT," POEMS (WRITTEN C. 1791-
1792) FROM *BLAKES'S NOTEBOOK*

. . . . .

There is no stopping place in this life—nor is there ever one
for any man, no matter how far along his way he's gone.

MEISTER ECKHART

. . . . .

We must, strictly speaking,
at every moment give each other up
and let each other go
and not hold each other back.

RANIER MARIA RILKE

. . . . .

This is the happiest of mortals, for he is above everything he
possesses.

VOLTAIRE (FRANÇOIS MARIE AROUET), *CANDIDE* (1759)

. . . . .

Art is long,
life short;
judgement difficult,
opportunity transient.

JOHANN WOLFGANG VON GOETHE, *WILHELM MEISTER'S APPRENTICESHIP* (1786-
1830), BK VII, CH 9

. . . . .

A talent is formed in stillness,
a character in the world's torrent.

JOHANN WOLFGANG VON GOETHE, *TORQUANTO TASSO* (1790), ACT I, SC II

. . . . .

It is not in the still calm of life, or in the repose of a pacific
station, that great characters are formed . . . . The habits of a
vigorous mind are formed in contending with difficulties. All
history will convince you of this, and that wisdom and
penetration are the fruit of experience, not the lesson of
retirement and leisure. Great necessities call out great virtues.

ABIGAL ADAMS, LETTER TO HER SON, JOHN QUINCY ADAMS (1780)

. . . . .

And deep distress hath humanized my Soul.

WILLIAM WORDSWORTH, "ELEGIAC STANZAS." *SUGGESTED BY A PICTURE OF PEELE CASTLE IN A STORM* (1807), ST. 9

. . . . .

Choose life, only that and always, and at whatever risk. To let
life leak out, or to let it wear away by the mere passage of time,
to withhold giving it and spending it, is to chose nothing.
Whatever you can do, or dream you can, begin it. Boldness has
genius, power and magic in it.

JOHANN GOETHE

. . . . .

Have courage for the great sorrows in life, and patience for the
small ones. And when you have laboriously accomplished your
daily task, go to sleep in peace. God is awake.

VICTOR HUGO

. . . . .

Courage! I have shown it for years; think you I shall lose it at
the moment when my sufferings are to end?

MARIE ANTOINETTE, ON THE WAY TO THE GUILLOTINE (1793)

. . . . .

Sorrows remembered sweeten present joy.

ROBERT POLLOCK, *THE COURSE OF TIME* (1827)

. . . . .

I have often observed that resignation is never so perfect as when the blessing denied begins to lose somewhat of its value in our eyes.

JANE AUSTEN, *PRIDE AND PREJUDICE* (1813)

. . . . .

We may draw good out of evil; we must not do evil, that good may come.

MARIA CHAPMAN, SPEECH (1855)

. . . . .

If there is something to pardon in everything, there is also something to condemn.

NIETZSCHE, *THE WILL TO POWER* (1888)

. . . . .

You shall have joy, or you shall have power, said God; you shall not have both.

RALPH WALDO EMERSON, *JOURNAL.* OCTOBER 1842

. . . . .

. . . he who remains passive when overwhelmed with grief loses his best chance of recovering elasticity of mind.

CHARLES DARWIN, *THE EXPRESSION OF EMOTION IN MAN AND ANIMALS*

. . . . .

'Tis dying—I am doing—but
I'm not afraid to know.

EMILY DICKINSON (1863), *POEMS, FIRST SERIES* (1890)

. . . . .

May I tell you why it seems to me a good thing for us to remember wrong that has been done to us? That we may forgive it.

CHARLES DICKENS

. . . . .

When I am dead, my dearest,
Sing no sad songs for me;
Plant thou no roses at my head,
Nor shady cypress tree:
Be the green grass above me
With showers and dewdrops wet;
And if thou wilt, remember,
And if thou wilt, forget.

CHRISTINA ROSSETTI, "SONG" (1848), *THE POETICAL WORKS OF CHRISTINA GEORGINA ROSSETTI* (1906)

. . . . .

Resolve to be thyself and know that he who finds himself loses his misery.

MATTHEW ARNOLD

. . . . .

Resolved, never to do anything which I should be afraid to do if it were the last hour of my life.

JONATHAN EDWARDS

. . . . .

Die when I may, I want it said of me by those who knew me best, that I always plucked a thistle and planted a flower where I thought the flower would grow.

ABRAHAM LINCOLN

. . . . .

The Heart asks Pleasure—first—
And then—Excuse from Pain—
And then—those little Anodynes
That deaden suffering—
And then—to go to sleep—
And then—if it should be
The will of its Inquisitor
The priviledge to die.

EMILY DICKINSON (1862), *POEMS FIRST SERIES* (1890), No. 536

. . . . .

I have got my leave.
Bid me farewell, my brothers!
I bow to you all and take my departure.
Here I give back the keys of my door—and I give up all claims to my house.
I only ask for last kind words from you.
We were neighbors for long, but I received more than I could give.
Now the day has dawned and the lamp that lit my dark corner is out.
A summons has come and I am ready for my journey.

TAGOR GITANJALI, XCIII

. . . . .

To be what we are, and to become what we are capable of becoming, is the only end of life.

ROBERT LOUIS STEVENSON, *FAMILIAR STUDIES OF MEN AND BOOKS* (1882)

. . . . .

Be not afraid of life.
Believe that life is worth living,
and your belief will help create the fact.

WILLIAM JAMES, *THE WILL TO BELIEVE* (1897), "IS LIFE WORTH LIVING?"

. . . . .

Live all you can;
It is a mistake not to.
It doesn't so much matter
What you do in particular,
So long as you have had your life.

HENRY JAMES

. . . . .

There are those who forget that death will come to all.
For those who remember, quarrels come to an end.

THE DHAMMAPADA

. . . . .

I leave this world without a regret.

HENRY DAVID THOREAU'S LAST WORDS

. . . . .

Turn up the lights. I don't want to go home in the dark.

O. HENRY'S LAST WORDS

. . . . .

Risk! Risk anything!
Care no more for the opinions of others.
Do the hardest thing on earth for you.
Act yourself. Face the truth.

KATERINE MANSFIELD (NEARING HER OWN DEATH)

. . . . .

Life shrinks or expands according to one's courage.

ANAIS NIN, (1941), THE DIARY OF ANAIS NIN, VOL. 3 (1969)

. . . . .

When our hope breaks,
Let our patience hold.

THOMAS FULLER

. . . . .

All truly wise thoughts have been thought already thousands
of times; but to make them truly ours, we must think them
over again honestly, till they take root in our personal
experience.

JOHANN WOLFGANG VON GOETHE

. . . . .

Great things are not made by impulse,
But by a series of small things brought together.

VINCENT VAN GOGH

. . . . .

To laugh often and much; to win the respect of intelligent
people and the affection of children; to earn the appreciation of
honest criticism and endure the betrayal of false friends; to
appreciate beauty and find the best in others; to leave the world
a bit better whether by a healthy child, a garden patch, a
redeemed social condition; to know even one life has breathed
easier because you have lived—this is to have succeeded.

RALPH WALDO EMERSON

. . . . .

The strongest principle of growth lies in human choice.

GEORGE ELLIOT, *DANIEL DERONDA* (1874)

. . . . .

We cannot freely and wisely choose the right way for ourselves
unless we know both good and evil.

HELEN KELLER, *MY RELIGION* (1927)

. . . . .

Happiness is beneficial for the body, but it is grief that
develops the powers of the mind.

MARCEL PROUST, *REMEMBRANCE OF THINGS PAST: THE PAST RECAPTURED* (1919)

. . . . .

Three failures denote uncommon strength.
A weakling has not enough grit to fail thrice.

MINNA THOMAS ANTRIM, *AT THE SIGN OF THE GOLDEN CALF* (1905)

. . . . .

We could never learn to be brave and patient, if there were only
joy in the world.

HELEN KELLER, IN *ATLANTIC MONTHY* (1890)

. . . . .

A little knowledge that acts is worth infinitely more than much
knowledge that is idle.

KAHLIL GIBRAN, *THE PROPHET*

. . . . .

'Tis dying—I am doing—
but I'm not afraid to know.

EMILY DICKINSON (1863), *POEMS, FIRST SERIES* (1890)

. . . . .

To grow, a lobster must shed its old shell numerous times.
Each shedding renders the creature totally defenseless until the
new shell forms . . . . There is risk in change. And risk can be
scary . . . . Change means uncertainty, but uncertainty breeds
opportunity . . . . When risk becomes frightening, think of the
lobster:
vulnerability is often the price of growth.

ANONYMOUS

. . . . .

Save us from weak resignation to violence,
teach us that restraint is the highest expression of power,
that thoughtfulness and tenderness are
the mark of the strong,
Help us to love our enemies,
not by countenancing their sins,
but remembering our own.

CHRISTIAN PRAYER

. . . . .

Beware of the man who does not return your blow;
he neither forgives you nor allows you to forgive yourself.

GEORGE BERNARD SHAW, *MAXIMS FOR REVOLUTIONISTS* (1903)

. . . . .

Courage is as often the outcome of despair as of hope; in the one
case we have nothing to lose, in the other everything to gain.

DIANE DE POITIERS, IN WINIFRED GORDON, *A BOOK OF DAYS* (1910)

.   .   .   .   .

The nearer she came to death, the more, by some perversity of nature, did she enjoy living.

ELLEN GLASGOW, *BARREN GROUND* (1925)

.   .   .   .   .

Such creatures of accident are we, liable to a thousand deaths before we are born. But once we are here, we may create our own world, if we choose.

MARY ANTIN, *THE PROMISED LAND* (1912)

.   .   .   .   .

If one burdens the future with one's worries,
it cannot grow organically.
I am filled with confidence,
not that I shall succeed in worldly things,
but that even when things go badly for me
I shall still find life good and worth living.

ETTY HILLESUM, *AN INTERRUPTED LIFE: THE DIARIES OF ETTY HILLESUM 1941-1943* (1983)

.   .   .   .   .

Misfortune had made Lilly supple instead of hardening her and a pliable substance is less easy to break than a stiff one.

EDITH WHARTON, *THE HOUSE OF MIRTH* (1905)

.   .   .   .   .

Knowledge of what you love somehows comes to you; you don't have to read nor analyze nor study. If you love a thing enough, knowledge of it seeps into you, with particulars more real than any chart can furnish.

JESSAMYN WEST, *THE FRIENDLY PERSUASION* (1940)

.   .   .   .   .

The leaves move in the garden, the sky is pale, and I catch myself weeping. It is hard—it is hard to make a good death.

KATHERINE MANSFIELD (1920), *JOURNAL OF KATHERINE MANSFIELD* (1930)

. . . . .

It is not dying, but living, that is a preparation for Death.

MARGOT ASQUITH, *MORE OR LESS ABOUT MYSELF* (1934)

. . . . .

You must do the thing you think you cannot do.

ELEANOR ROOSEVELT

. . . . .

No one can make you feel inferior without your consent.

ELEANOR ROOSEVELT, *THIS IS MY STORY* (1937)

. . . . .

There is plenty of courage among us for the abstract but not
for the concrete.

HELEN KELLER, *LET US HAVE FAITH* (1940)

. . . . .

Life is either a daring adventure, or nothing.

HELEN KELLER

. . . . .

God asks no person
Whether they will accept life.
That is not the choice.
You must take it.
The only choice is how.

HENRY WARD BEECHER

. . . . .

I think that the dying pray at the last not "please," but "thank
you," as a guest thanks his host at the door. Falling from
airplanes the people are crying thank you, thank you, all down
the air; and the cold carriages draw up for them on the rocks.

ANNIE DILLARD, *PILGRIM AT TINKER CREEK* (1974)

. . . . .

Tenderness contains an element of sadness. It is not the sadness of feeling sorry for yourself or feeling deprived but it is a natural situation of fullness. You feel so full and rich, as if you were about to shed tears. Your eyes are full of tears, and the moment you blink, the tears will spill out of your eyes and roll down your cheeks. In order to be a good warrior, one has to feel this sad and tender heart. If a person does not feel alone and sad, he cannot be a warrior at all.

CHØGYAM TRUNGPA, *SHAMBAHALA: THE SACRED PATH OF THE WARRIOR*

. . . . .

Let me not pray to be sheltered from dangers,
But to be fearless in facing them.

Let me not beg for the stilling of my pain,
But for the heart to conquer it.

Let me not look for allies in life's battlefield,
But to my own strength.

Let me not crave in anxious fear to be saved,
But hope for the patience to win my freedom.

Grant me that I may not be a coward,
feeling your mercy in my success alone,
But let me find the grasp of your hand in my failure.

RABINDRANATH TAGORE

. . . . .

It isn't for the moment you are struck that you need courage but for the long uphill climb back to sanity and faith and security.

ANNE MORROW LINDBERGH, (1932), *HOUR OF GOLD, HOUR OF LEAD*, (1973)

. . . . .

Birth is the starting point of passion.
Passion is the beginning of death.
How can you turn back from birth?
How can you say no to passion?
How can you bid death hold off?
And if thoughts come and hold you
And if dreams step in and shake your bones
What can you do but take them and
    make them
    more your own?

CARL SANDBURG, "FOG NUMBERS," *HONEY AND SALT*

. . . . .

I still grieve for the words unsaid.
Something terrible happens
when we stop the mouths of the dying before they are dead.
A silence grows up between us then,
profounder than the grave.
If we force the dying to go speechless,
the stone dropped in the well will fall forever
before the answering splash is heard.

FAYE MOSKOWITZ, *A LEAK IN THE HEART* (1985)

. . . . .

One cannot be honest even at the end of one's life,
for no one is wholly alone.
We are bound to those we love,
or to those who love us,
and to those who need us to be brave, or content,
or even happy enough to allow them not to worry about us.
So we must refrain from giving pain,
as our last gift to our fellows.

FLORIDA SCOTT-MAXWELL, *THE MEMORIES OF MY DAYS* (1968)

. . . . .

When one is a stranger to oneself then one is estranged from others too. If one is out of touch with oneself, then one cannot touch others.

ANNE MORROW LINDBERGH, *GIFT FROM THE SEA* (1955)

. . . . .

Freedom means choosing your burden.

HEPHZIBAH MENUHIN

. . . . .

We have to be utterly broken before we can realize it is impossible to better the truth. It is the truth that we deny which so tenderly and forgivingly picks up the fragments and puts them together again.

LAURENS VAN DER POST

. . . . .

Work is love made visible. And if you cannot work with love but only with distaste, it is better that you should leave your work and sit at the gate of the temple and take alms of those who work with joy. For if you bake bread with indifference, you bake bitter bread that feeds but half man's hunger.

KAHLIL GIBRAN, *THE PROPHET*

. . . . .

Nothing worth doing is completed in our lifetime;
Therefore we are saved by hope.
Nothing true or beautiful or good makes complete sense in any immediate context of history;
Therefore we are saved by faith.
Nothing we do, however virtuous, can be accomplished alone;
Therefore we are saved by love.
No virtuous act is quite as virtuous from the standpoint of our friend of foe as from our own;
Therefore we are saved by the final form of love which is forgiveness.

REINHOLD NIEBUHR, *THE IRONY OF AMERICAN HISTORY* (1952)

. . . . .

There are no true beginnings but in pain.
When you understand that and can withstand pain,
then you're almost ready to start.

LESLIE WOOLF HEDLEY

. . . . .

Transcendence or detachment, leaving the body, pure love, lack
of jealousy—that's the vision we are given by our culture,
generally when we think of the highest thing . . . . Another way
to look at it is that the aim of the person is not to be detached,
but to be more attached—to be attached to working; to be
attached to making chairs or something that helps everyone; to
be attached to beauty; to be attached to music.

ROBERT BLY

. . . . .

I decided to start anew—to strip away what I had been taught,
to accept as true my own thinking. This was one of the best
times of my life. There was no one around to look at what I
was doing, no one interested, no one to say anything about it
one way or another. I was alone and singularly free, working
into my own, unknown—no one to satisfy but myself. I began
with charcoal and paper and decided not to use any color until
it was impossible to do what I wanted to do in black and white.
I believe it was June before I needed blue.

GEORGIA O'KEEFE

. . . . .

To endure oneself may be the hardest task in the universe.

FRANK HERBERT, DUNE MESSIAH (1998)

. . . . .

One can never pay in gratitude; one can only "pay in kind"
somewhere else in life.

ANNE MORROW LINDBERGH

. . . . .

One can give nothing whatever without giving oneself—that is to say, risking oneself. If one cannot risk oneself, then one is simply incapable of giving.

JAMES BALDWIN, *THE FIRE NEXT TIME* (1964)

. . . . .

It is the process of accumulation that creates habit, imitation, and for the mind that accumulates there is deterioration, death. But a mind that is not accumulating, not gathering, that is dying each day, each minute—for such a mind there is no death. It is in a state of infinite space. So the mind must die to everything it has gathered—to all the habits, the imitated virtues, to all the things it has relied upon for its sense of security. Then it is no longer caught in the net of its own thinking. In dying to the past from moment to moment the mind is made fresh, therefore it can never deteriorate or set in motion the wave of darkness.

J. KRISHNAMURTI, *THINK ON THESE THINGS* (1984)

. . . . .

A life spent making mistakes
Is not only more honorable but more useful
Than a life doing nothing.

GEORGE BERNARD SHAW

. . . . .

Faith took her deep into the woods,
Sat her down,
And asked her to follow her heart.

MELISSA HARRIS

. . . . .

Courage is the price that
Life exacts for granting peace.

AMELIA EARHART, *COURAGE* (1927)

. . . . .

Every once in a while I awaken to the reality that I'm all I've got.

CLARK MOUSTAKAS (1963)

. . . . .

Learn to forgive yourself again
   ... and again
      ... and again

SHELDON KOPP, *NO HIDDEN MEANINGS* (1975)

. . . . .

It takes far less courage to kill yourself than it takes to make yourself wake up one more time.

JUDITH ROSSNER, *NINE MONTHS IN THE LIFE OF AN OLD MAID* (1969)

. . . . .

But understanding alone is not enough. When I understand something and do not put this into action, nothing has been accomplished either in the outside world or within myself. . . . when I was being my own therapist I hit on something that was really blocking me and kept telling myself that as long as this was clear to me, as long as I understood how it had come about, I didn't need to do anything about it. "It's all right."

It wasn't. Nothing happened until I acted on what I knew. It seems to be one of the follies of my intellect that it can think that what I know I am, and that words take care of everything.

CARL ROGERS AND BARRY STEVENS, *PERSON TO PERSON* (1973)

. . . . .

The last time you're doing something—knowing you're doing it for the last—makes it even more alive than the first.

GLORIA NAYLOR, *MAMA DAY* (1988)

. . . . .

We begin to see that the completion of an important project has every right to be dignified by a natural grieving process. Something that required the best of us has ended. We will miss it.

ANNE WILSON SCHAEF, *MEDITATIONS FOR WOMEN WHO DO TOO MUCH* (1990)

. . . . .

Mourning . . . is an undoing. Every minute tie has to be untied and something permanent and valuable recovered and assimilated from the knot. The end is gain, of course. Blessed are they that mourn, for they shall be made strong, in fact. But the process is like all human births, painful and long and dangerous.

MARGERY ALLINGHAM

. . . . .

A poem . . . begins as a lump in the throat, a sense of wrong, a homesickness, a love sickness . . . . It finds the thought and the thought finds the words.

ROBERT FROST

. . . . .

The life we want is not merely the one we have chosen and made; it is the one we must be choosing and making. To keep it alive we must be perpetually choosing it and making its differences from among all contrary and alternative possibilities. We must accept the pain and labor of that, or we lose its satisfactions and its joy. Only by risking it, offering it freely to its possibilities, can we keep it.

WENDELL BERRY, *A CONTINUOUS HARMONY* (1972)

. . . . .

A sheltered life can be a daring one as well. For all serious daring starts from within.

EUDORA WELTY, *ONE WRITER'S BEGINNINGS* (1984), "FINDING A VOICE"

.   .   .   .   .

Finally, you see that there is nothing you can trust—nobody, no authority—except the process itself. Finally the trust is . . . trusting reality. It is just trust—confidence in the essence itself.

A. H. ALMAAS

.   .   .   .   .

This path is difficult because it has not been carved; and it has not been carved because I have not lived before.

SALLY PALAIN

.   .   .   .   .

In all men is evil sleeping; the good man is he who will not awaken it, in himself or in other men.

MARY RENAULT, THE PRAISE SINGER (1978)

.   .   .   .   .

Flops are a part of life's menu and I'm never a girl to miss out on any of the courses.

ROSALIND RUSSELL, IN BARBARA MCDOWELL AND HANA UMLAUF, WOMAN'S ALMANAC (1977)

.   .   .   .   .

If you have made mistakes, even serious ones, there is always another chance for you. What we call failure is not the falling down, but the staying down.

MARY PICKFORD, IN READER'S DIGEST (1979)

.   .   .   .   .

And I believe that I will never be able to hate any human being for his so called "wickedness," that I shall only hate the evil that is within me, though hate is perhaps putting it too strongly even then. In any case, we cannot be lax enough in what we demand of others and strict enough in what we demand of ourselves.

ETTY HILLESUM, AN INTERRUPTED LIFE: THE DIARIES OF ETTY HILLESUM 1941-1943 (1983)

. . . . .

You cannot make yourself feel something you do not feel, but you can make yourself do right in spite of your feelings.

PEARL BUCK, *TO MY DAUGHTERS, WITH LOVE* (1967)

. . . . .

I don't know what will happen now. We've got some difficult days ahead. But it really doesn't matter to me now, because I've been to the mountaintop. And I don't mind. Like anyone, I would like to live a long life; longevity has its place. But I'm not concerned about that now. I just want to do God's will. And he's allowed me to go up to the mountain. And I've looked over. And I've seen the promised land. I may not get there with you. But I want you to know tonight that we as a people will get to the promised land. And I'm happy tonight. I'm not worried about anything. I'm not fearing any man. Mine eyes have seen the glory of the coming of the Lord!

MARTIN LUTHER KING, JR., "I'VE BEEN TO THE MOUNTAINTOP" SPEECH ON THE EVE OF HIS ASSASSINATION, APRIL 3, 1968.

. . . . .

Darkness cannot drive out darkness; only light can do that. Hate cannot drive out hate; only love can do that . . . The chain reaction of evil—hate begetting hate, wars producing more wars—must be broken, or we shall be plunged into the abyss of annihilation.

MARTIN LUTHER KING, JR., *STRENGTH TO LOVE* (1963)

. . . . .

Mourning does not achieve the goal of separating the mourner, and by arriving at a river of forgetfulness, from the company of the dead . . . both mourning and life review make use of recurring reminiscences to manifest and affirm the experience of continuity.

MARK KAMINSKI, *THE USES OF REMINISCENCE*

. . . . .

If, after all, we cannot always make history have a meaning, we can always act so that our own lives have one.

ALBERT CAMUS

. . . . .

I do not want to die . . . until I have faithfully made the most of my talent and cultivated the seed that was placed in me until the last small twig had grown.

KÄTHE KOLLWITZ (1915), IN HANS KOLLWITZ, ED., *THE DIARIES AND LETTERS OF KÄTHE KOLLWITZ* (1955)

. . . . .

Unless I am what I am and feel what I feel — as hard as I can and as honestly as truly as I can — then I am nothing. Let me feel guilty . . . don't try to educate me . . . don't try to protect me.

ELIZABETH JANEWAY, *LEAVING HOME* (1953)

. . . . .

I think one should forgive and remember . . . If you forgive and forget, you're just driving what you remember into the subconscious; it stays there and festers. But to look, even regularly, upon what you remember and know you've forgiven is an achievement.

FAITH BALDWIN

. . . . .

. . . the most famous of the unfinished situations is the fact that we have not forgiven our parents.

FRITZ PERLS

. . . . .

I want to know that the step I take is real, that my heartbeat is its own, that my words belong to me, that my ideals have a place in reality.

CLARK MOUSTAKAS, *LONELINESS AND LOVE*

. . . . .

I do not believe that sheer suffering teaches. If suffering alone taught then all the world would be wise, since everyone suffers. To suffering must be added mourning, understanding, patience, love, openness, and the willingness to remain vulnerable.

ANNE MORROW LINDBERGH, *HOUR OF GOLD, HOUR OF LEAD*

. . . . .

The amazing process . . . begins with the decision not to fight against our vices, not to run away from them nor conceal them, but to bring them into the light. If the desire to be honest is greater than the desire to be good or bad, then the terrific power of our vices will become manifest, and behind the vice the old forgotten fear will turn up (the fear of being excluded from life), and behind the fear the pain (the pain of not being loved), and behind the pain of loneliness the deepest and most powerful and most hidden of all human desires: the desire to love, to give oneself, and to be a part of the living stream that we call brotherhood.

FRITZ KUNKEL

. . . . .

We who lived in concentration camps can remember the men who walked through the huts comforting others, giving away their last piece of bread. They may have been few in number, but they offer sufficient proof that everything can be taken away from man but one thing: the last of human freedoms—to choose one's attitude in any given set of circumstances, to choose one's way.

VIKTOR FRANKL

. . . . .

There is a law so cruel and so just which demands that one must grow or else pay more for staying the same.

NORMAN MAILER, *THE DEER PARK*

. . . . .

I would like to believe when I die that I have given myself away
like a tree that sows seed every spring and never counts the
loss, because it is not loss, it is adding to future life. It is the
tree's way of being. Strongly rooted perhaps, but spilling out its
treasure on the wind.

MAY SARTON, *RECOVERING: A JOURNAL* (1978-1979)

. . . . .

If I knew for certain that I should die next week, I would still
be able to sit at my desk all week and study with perfect
equanimity, for I know now that life and death make a
meaningful whole.

ETTY HILLESUM, *AN INTERRUPTED LIFE: THE DIARIES OF ETTY HILLESUM 1941-
1943* (1983)

. . . . .

Coming to the end of spring
my grandmother kicks off her shoes
steps out of her faltering body.

BETSY SHOLL, "SPRING FRAGMENTS," *ROOMS OVERHEAD* (1986)

. . . . .

Don't be dismayed at good-byes.
A farewell is necessary before you can meet again.
And meeting again, after moments or lifetimes,
is certain for those who are friends.

RICHARD BACH

. . . . .

 I have decided to stick with love.
Hate is too great a burden to bear.

MARTIN LUTHER KING, JR.

. . . . .

You must not change one thing, one pebble, one grain of sand,
until you know what good and evil will follow on that act.

URSULA K. LE GUIN, *A WIZARD OF EARTHSEA* (1968)

. . . . .

Growth is optional.
Not all will choose it.
Growth means becoming more of who we already are,
not what others want us to be.
Growth means evolving and waking up,
not remaining asleep in the illusions of the learned self.

BRENDA SCHAEFFER

. . . . .

A person can run for years but soon or later he has to take a
stand in the place which, for better or worse, he calls home, do
what he can to change things there.

PAULE MARSHALL, "THE CHOSEN PLACE," THE TIMELESS PEOPLE (1969)

. . . . .

Character cannot be developed in ease and quiet. Only
through experience of trial and suffering can the soul be
strengthened, vision cleared, ambition inspired, and success
achieved.

HELEN KELLER, HELEN KELLER'S JOURNAL (1938)

. . . . .

Mourning is not forgetting . . . It is an undoing. Every minute
tie has to be untied and something permanent and valuable
recovered and assimilated from the dust.

MARGERY ALLINGTON, THE TIGER IN THE SMOKE (1952)

. . . . .

Dying was apparently a weaning process; all the attachments to
familiar people and objects had to be undone.

LISA ALTHER, KINFLICKS (1975)

. . . . .

Life had taught him that the unforgivable was usually the most
easily forgiven.

P. D. JAMES, DEATH OF AN EXPERT WITNESS (1977)

. . . . .

Writers seldom choose as friends those self-contained
characters who are never in trouble, never unhappy or ill, never
make mistakes, and always count their change when it is
handed to them.

CATHERINE DRINKER BOWEN, IN *ATLANTIC* (1957)

. . . . .

Pain comes from experiencing life just as it is, with no
trimmings. We can even call this direct experiencing joy. But
when we try to run away and escape from our experience of
pain, we suffer. Freedom is the willingness to risk being
vulnerable to life.

CHARLOTTE JOKO BECK

. . . . .

Looking down into my father's dead face for the last time my
mother said without tears, without smiles without regrets but
with civility

"Goodnight, Willie Lee, I'll see you in the morning."

And it was then I knew that the healing of all our wounds is
forgiveness that permits a promiseof our return at the end.

ALICE WALKER, *GOODNIGHT WILLIE LEE, I'LL SEE YOU IN THE MORNING*

. . . . .

An individual who breaks the law that conscience tells him is
unjust, and who willingly accepts the penalty of imprisonment
in order to arouse the conscience of the community over its
injustice, is in reality expressing the highest respect for the law.

MARTIN LUTHER KING, JR.

. . . . .

It is good to have an end to journey towards;
but it is the journey that matters in the end.

URSULA K. LE GUIN, *THE LEFT HAND OF DARKNESS* (1969)

．　．　．　．　．

The problem is . . . basically: how to remain whole in the midst
of the distractions of life; how to remain balanced, no matter
what centrifugal forces tend to pull one off center; how to
remain strong, no matter what shocks come at the periphery
and tend to crack the hub of the wheel.

ANNE MORROW LINDBERGH

．　．　．　．　．

All important decisions must be made on the basis of
insufficient information.

SHELDON KOPP, *No Hidden Meanings*

．　．　．　．　．

Once the meaning of suffering had been revealed to us, we
refused to minimize or alleviate the camp's tortures by ignoring
them or harbouring false illusions and entertaining artificial
optimism. Suffering has become a task on which we did not
want to turn our backs . . . it was necessary to face up to the full
amount of suffering, trying to keep moments of weakness and
furtive tears to a minimum.

But there was no need to be ashamed of tears, for tears bore
witness that a man had the greatest of courage, the courage to
suffer. Only very few realized that.

VICTOR FRANKL, *Man's Search for Meaning*

．　．　．　．　．

The world breaks everyone and afterwards many are strong at
the broken places.

ERNEST HEMINGWAY

．　．　．　．　．

The ultimate measure of a person is not where they stand in
moments of comfort and convenience, but where they stand at
times of challenge and controversy.

MARTIN LUTHER KING, JR.

. . . . .

To confront a person with his own shadow is to show him his
own light.

CARL JUNG

. . . . .

Dying
Is an art, like everything else.
I do it exceptionally well.

SYLVIA PLATH, "LADY LAZARUS," *ARIEL* (1965)

. . . . .

i thank You God for this most amazing
day: for the leaping greenly spirits of trees
and a blue true dream of sky, and for everything
which is natural which is infinite
which is yes

(i who have died am alive again today,
and this is the sun's birthday, this is the birth
day of life and of love and wings:
and of the gay
great happening illimitably earth)

how should touching tasting touching hearing seeing
breathing any—lifted from the no
of all nothing—human merely being
doubt imaginable you?

(now the ears of my ears awake
and
now the eyes of my eyes are opened)

EE CUMMINGS

. . . . .

I have died so little today, my friend, forgive me.

THOMAS LUX

. . . . .

Love cannot remain by itself—it has no meaning.
Love has to be put into action and that action is service.

Whatever form we are, able or disabled, rich or poor,
it is not how much we do, but how much love we put into the
doing, a lifelong sharing of love with others.

MOTHER TERESA, *A LIFELONG SHARING*

. . . . .

People say, what is the sense of our small effort. They cannot
see that we must lay one brick at a time, take one step at a time.
A pebble cast into a pond causes ripples that spread in all
directions. Each one of our thoughts, words and deeds are like
that. No one has a right to sit down and feel hopeless. There's
too much work to do.

DOROTHY DAY, *COMMITMENT*

. . . . .

To be born is to start the journey towards death.

MADELEINE L'ENGLE, *WALKING ON WATER: REFLECTIONS ON FAITH AND ART* (1980)

. . . . .

Look at every path closely and deliberately. Try it as many
times as you think necessary. Then ask yourself, and yourself
alone, one question. Does the path have a heart? The trouble is
nobody asks the question; and when a man finally realizes that
he has taken a path without a heart, the path is ready to kill
him. At that point, very few men can stop to deliberate and
leave the path.

DON JUAN, IN CARLOS CASTANADA, *THE TEACHINGS OF DON JUAN*

. . . . .

There is often in people to whom "the worst" has happened an
almost transcendent freedom, for they have faced "the worst"
and survived it.

CAROL PEARSON, *THE HERO WITHIN* (1986)

· · · · ·

History, despite its wrenching pain
Cannot be unlived, but if faced
With courage, need not be lived again.

MAYA ANGELOU, "ON THE PULSE OF MORNING," PRESIDENT CLINTON
INAGURAL, 1992

· · · · ·

But I'm getting ready to go. How am I doin' it? I'm layin' aside
every weight and a sin that does so easily beset me and I'm
gettin' light for the flight.

WILLIE MAE FORD SMITH, IN BRIAN LANKER, *I DREAM A WORLD* (1989)

· · · · ·

That is what they call being reconciled to die. They call it
reconciled when pain has strummed a symphony of suffering
back and forth across you, up and down, round and round you
until each little fiber is worn tissue-thin with aching. And
when you are lying beaten, and buffeted, battered and
broken—pain goes out, joins hands with Death and comes
back to dance, dance, dance, stamp, stamp down on you until
you give up.

MARITA BONNER, "A POSSIBLE TRIAD ON BLACK NOTES" (1933), *FRYE STREET
AND ENVIRONS* (1987)

· · · · ·

There is only one thing pain is good for. It teaches you to love.
God bless pain.

JOEY GOLDFARB

· · · · ·

When anyone seriously pursues an art—painting, poetry,
sculpture, composing—over twenty or thirty years, the
sustained discipline carries the artist down to the countryside
of grief; and that descent, resisted so long, proves invigorating .
. . . As I've gotten older, I find I am able to be nourished more
by sorrow and to distinguish it from depression.

ROBERT BLY

. . . . .

Give your sorrow all the space and shelter in yourself that is its due, for if everyone bears his grief honestly and courageously, the sorrow that now fills the world will abate. But if you do not clear a decent shelter for your sorrow, and instead reserve most of the space inside you for hatred and thoughts of revenge — from which new sorrows will be born for others — then sorrow will never cease in this world and will multiply.

ETTY HILLESUM, *AN INTERRUPTED LIFE: THE DIARIES OF ETTY HILLESUM 1941-1943* (1983)

. . . . .

The ability to choose puts human beings in control of their actions. Implied in choice is that the action taken is best, and that all other actions are overruled. We cannot knowingly choose what is not good for us. The ability to pursue a course, whether it is a popular one or not, is measured in courage. The greater the courage, the greater the possibility we will act for change. I build my characters around the dynamics of choice, courage and change.

MILDRED PITTS WALTER, *THE HORN BOOK* (1991)

. . . . .

We cannot influence death, but we can influence the style of our departure. Men surprise themselves by the fashion in which they face this death; some more proudly and valiantly than ever they dared imagine; and some in abject terror.

CYRSU L. SULZBURG, *MY BROTHER DEATH*

. . . . .

 Because grief may become a substitute for the dead one, giving up our grief can be the greatest challenge of mourning.

MARY JANE MOFFAT, *IN THE MIDST OF WINTER* (1982)

Rethinking and Self-Empowerment

. . . .

For in much wisdom is much grief:
and he that increaseth knowledge increaseth sorrow.

ECCLESIASTICS 1:18

. . . .

Not life, but good life, is to be chiefly valued.

SOCRATES

. . . .

Whoever destroys a single life is as guilty
as though he had destroyed the entire world;
and whoever rescues a single life earns
as much merit as though he had rescued the entire world.

TALMUD (COMPILED C. 6TH CENTURY A.D.), MISHNA. SANHEDRIN

. . . .

To yield is to be preserved whole.
To be bent is to become straight.
To be empty is to be full.
To be worn out is to be renewed.
To have little is to possess.
To have plenty is to be perplexed.

LAO-TZU (C. 604-C. 531 B.C.), THE WAY OF LAO-TZU, 22

. . . .

There are three truths:
my truth, your truth and the truth.

CHINESE PROVERB

. . . . .

The softest things in the world overcome the hardest things in
the world. Non-being penetrates that in which there is no
space. Through this I know the advantage of taking no action.

LAO-TZU (C. 604-C. 531 B.C.), *THE WAY OF LAO-TZU*, 43

. . . . .

True words are not beautiful;
Beautiful words are not true.
A good man does not argue;
He who argues is not a good man.
A wise man has no extensive knowledge;
He who has extensive knowledge is not a wise man.
The sage does not accumulate for himself.
The more he uses for others, the more he has himself.
The more he gives to others, the more he possess of his own.
The Way of Heaven is to benefit others and not to injure.
The Way of the sage is to act but not to compete.

LAO-TZU (C. 604-C.531 B.C.), *THE WAY OF LAO-TZU*, 81

. . . . .

Even his griefs are a joy long after to one that remembers all
that he wrought and endured.

HOMER (C. 700 B.C.), *ODYSSEY*, BK. XV, L. 400

. . . . .

Have no friends not equal to yourself.

CONFUCIUS (551-479 B.C.), *THE CONFUCIAN ANALECTS*, BK. 1:8, III

. . . . .

Opposites are cures for opposites.

HIPPOCRATES (C. 460-377 B.C.), *BREATHS*, BK. I

. . . . .

And be not conformed to this world:
but be ye transformed by the renewing of your mind.

ROMANS 12:2

．　．　．　．　．

I know nothing except the fact of my ignorance.

SOCRATES (469-399 B.C.), IN DIOGENES LAERTIUS, *LIVES OF EMINENT PHILOSOPHERS*, BK. II, SEC. 32

．　．　．　．　．

The wise learn many things from their enemies.

ARISTOPHANES, *BIRDS* (414 B.C.), L. 375

．　．　．　．　．

No human thing is of serious importance.

PLATO (C. 428-348 B.C.), *THE REPUBLIC*, BK. X, 604-C

．　．　．　．　．

What is a friend?
A single soul dwelling in two bodies.

ARISTOTLE (384-322 B.C.), IN DIOGENES LAERTIUS, *LIVES OF EMINENT PHILOSOPHERS*, BK. V, SEC. 20

．　．　．　．　．

There are occasions when it is undoubtedly better
to incur loss than to make gain.

TITUS MACCIUS PLAUTUS (254-184 B.C.), *CAPTIVI*, ACT II, SC. II, L. 77

．　．　．　．　．

I have everything, yet have nothing;
and although I possess nothing,
still of nothing am I in want.

TERENCE (PUBLIUS TERENTIUS AFER) (C. 190-159 B.C.), *EUNUCHUS*, L. 243

．　．　．　．　．

The best ideas are common property.

LUCIUS ANNAEUS SENECA (8 B.C.-A.D. 65), *EPISTLES 12, 11*

．　．　．　．　．

A good mind possesses a kingdom.

LUCIUS ANNAEUS SENECA (8 B.C.-A.D. 65), *THYESTES 380*

. . . . .

In fact, nothing is said that has not been said before.

TERENCE (PUBLIUS TERENTIUS AFER) (C. 190-159 B.C.), *EUNUCHUS*, L. 41
(PROLOGUE)

. . . . .

What was hard to bear is sweet to remember.

PORTUGUESE PROVERB

. . . . .

We should not moor a ship with one anchor,
Or our life with one hope.

EPICTETUS

. . . . .

The king has been very good to me.
He promoted me from a simple maid to be a marchioness.
Then he raised me to be a queen.
Now he will raise me to be a martyr.

ANNE BOLEYN (1536), IN WILLIS J. ABBOTT, *NOTABLE WOMEN IN HISTORY*
(1913)

. . . . .

To do a great right, do a little wrong.

WILLIAM SHAKESPEARE, *THE MERCHANT OF VENICE* (1596-1597), ACT IV, SC. I,
L. 216

. . . . .

What's mine is yours, and what is yours is mine.

WILLIAM SHAKESPEARE, *MEASURE FOR MEASURE* (1604-1605), ACT V, SC. I, L. 539

. . . . .

Poor and content is rich, and rich enough.

WILLIAM SHAKESPEARE, *OTHELLO* (1604-1605), ACT III, SC. III, L. 172

. . . . .

Music to hear, why hear'st thou music sadly?
Sweets with sweet war not, joy delights in joy.

WILLIAM SHAKESPEARE, *SONNET 8* (PUBLISHED 1609), L. 1

. . . . .

And ruin'd love, when it is built anew,
Grows fairer than at first, more strong, far greater.

WILLIAM SHAKESPEARE, *SONNET 119* (PUBLISHED 1609), L. 11

. . . . .

Give every man thine ear, but few thy voice,
Take each man's censure, but reserve thy judgment.
Costly thy habit as thy purse can buy,
But not expressed in fancy; rich not gaudy;
For the apparel oft proclaims the man,

Neither a borrower, nor a lender be;
For the loan oft loses both itself and friend,
And borrowing dulls the edge of husbandry,
This above all; to thine own self be true,
And it must follow, as the night the day,
Thou canst not then be false to any man.

WILLIAM SHAKESPEARE, *HAMLET* (1600-1601), ACT I, SC. III, L. 75

. . . . .

No rule is so general,
which admits not some exception.

ROBERT BURTON, "DEMOCRITUS TO THE READER," PT. I, SEC. 2, MEMBER 1,
SUBSEC. 3, *ANATOMY OF MELANCHOLY* (1621-1651)

. . . . .

If your reputation is ruined—might as well have fun.

OLD GERMAN PROVERB

No light, but rather darkness visible.

JOHN MILTON, *PARADISE LOST* (1667) BK. I, L. 63

A mind not to be chang'd by place or time.
The mind is its own place, and in itself
Can make a heav'n of hell, a hell of heav'n.

JOHN MILTON, *PARADISE LOST* (1667) BK. I, L. 253

One cannot conceive anything so strange and so implausible
that it has not already been said by one philosopher or another.

RENÉ DESCARTES, *LE DISCOURS DE LA MÉTHODE* (1637), II

Who lives without folly is not so wise as he thinks.

FRANÇOIS, DUC DE LA ROCHEFOUCAULD, *REFLECTIONS; OR, SENTENCES AND MORAL MAXIMS*, (1678), 209

Pleasure is nothing else but the intermission of pain.

JOHN SELDEN, "PLEASURE," *TABLE TALK* (1689)

Wise men say nothing in dangerous times.

JOHN SELDON, "WISDOM," *TABLE TALK* (1689)

Change everything, except your loves.

VOLTAIRE (FRANÇOIS MARIE AROUET) (1694-1778), *SUR L'USAGE DE LA VIE*

A little learning is a dangerous thing;
Drink deep, or taste not the Pierian spring:
There shallow draughts intoxicate the brain,
And drinking largely sobers us again.

ALEXANDER POPE, *AN ESSAY ON CRITICISM* (1711), PT. II, L. 15

. . . . .

Liberty of thought is the life of the soul.

> Voltaire (François Marie Arouet) (1694-1778), Essay on Epic Poetry

. . . . .

You purchase pain with all that joy can give,
And die of nothing but a rage to live.

> Alexander Pope, "Epistle II, To Mrs. M. Blount" (1735), l. 95, Moral Essays (1731-1735)

. . . . .

Work as if you were to live a hundred years,
Pray as if you were to die tomorrow.

> Benjamin Franklin, Poor Richard's Almanac (May, 1757)

. . . . .

This world is a comedy to those that think,
a tragedy to those that feel.

> Horace Walpole, Letters. To the Countess of Upper Ossory (August 16, 1776)

. . . . .

One never goes so far as when one doesn't know where one is going.

> Johann Wolfgang von Goethe, letter to Karl Friedrich Zelter (December 3, 1812)

. . . . .

Dost thou love life?
Then do not squander time,
for that's the stuff life is made of.

> Benjamin Franklin, Poor Richard's Almanac (June, 1746)

. . . . .

I love those who yearn for the impossible.

> Johann Wolfgang von Goethe, "The Second Part, act II, Classical Walpurgis Night," Faust (1808-1832)

. . . . .

Everything that emancipates the spirit without giving us control over ourselves is harmful.

JOHANN WOLFGANG VON GOETHE (1749-1832), *PROVERBS IN PROSE*

. . . . .

He who has done his best for his own time has lived for all times.

JOHANN CHRISTOPH FRIEDRICH VON SCHILLER, *WALLENSTEIN'S CAMP* (1798), PROLOGUE

. . . . .

But people themselves alter so much, that there is something new to be observed in them forever.

JANE AUSTEN, *PRIDE AND PREJUDICE* (1813)

. . . . .

We feel that we are greater than we know.

WILLIAM WORDSWORTH, *THE RIVER DUDDON* (1820), SONNET 34, AFTERTHOUGHT, L. 14

. . . . .

A deep distress hath humanized my Soul.

WILLIAM WORDSWORTH, ELEGIAC STANZAS. *SUGGESTED BY A PICTURE OF PEELE CASTLE IN A STORM* (1807), ST. 9

. . . . .

Society everywhere is in conspiracy against the personhood of everyone of its members . . . . The virtue in most request is conformity. Self-reliance is its aversion.

RALPH WALDO EMERSON, "SELF-RELIANCE," *ESSAYS: FIRST SERIES* (1841)

. . . . .

Whoso would be a man must be a non-conformist.

RALPH WALDO EMERSON, "SELF-RELIANCE," *ESSAYS: FIRST SERIES* (1841)

. . . . .

[Imagination] reveals itself in the balance or reconciliation of
opposite or discordant qualities:of sameness, with difference;
of the general, with the concrete; the idea, with the image; the
individual, with the representative; the sense of novelty and
freshness, with old and familiar objects; a more than usual state
of emotion, with more than usual order; judgment ever awake
and steady self-possession, with enthusiasm and feeling
profound or vehement; and while it blends and harmonizes the
natural and the artificial, still subordinates art to nature; the
manner to the matter; and our admiration of the poet to our
sympathy with the poetry.

SAMUEL TAYLOR COLERIDGE, *BIOGRAPHIA LITERATIA* (1817)

. . . . .

To believe your own thought, to believe that what is true for
you in your private heart true for all men—that is genius.

RALPH WALDO EMERSON, "SELF-RELIANCE," *ESSAYS: FIRST SERIES* (1841).

. . . . .

This time, like all times, is a very good one, if we but know
what to do with it.

RALPH WALDO EMERSON, *MAN THINKING: THE AMERICAN SCHOLAR* (1837),
SEC. 3

. . . . .

He is not dead! he only left
A precious robe of clay behind,
To draw a robe of love and light
Around his disembodied mind.

FRANCES ELLEN WATKINS HARPER, OBITUARY FOR J. EDWARDS BARNES, IN
NATIONAL ANTI-SLAVERY STANDARD (1858)

. . . . .

Because I could not stop for Death
He kindly stopped for me
The Carriage held but just Ourselves
And Immortality.

EMILY DICKINSON, #712 (WRITTEN C. 1863, PUBLISHED 1890), ST. 1

. . . . .

In the first moment when we come away from the presence of
death, every other relation to the living is merged, to our
feeling, in the great relation of a common nature and a
common destiny.

GEORGE ELIOT, THE LIFTED VEIL (1859)

. . . . .

If a man does not keep pace with his companions, perhaps it is
because he hears a different drummer. Let him step to the
music which he hears, however measured or far away.

HENRY DAVID THOREAU, WALDEN (1854)

. . . . .

If a little knowledge is dangerous, where is the man who has so
much as to be out of danger?

THOMAS HENRY HUXLEY, ON ELEMENTAL INSTRUCTION IN PHYSIOLOGY (1877)

. . . . .

If one advances confidently in the direction of his dreams, and
endeavors to live the life which he has imagined, he will meet
with a success unexpected in common hours. He will put some
things behind, will pass an invisible boundary . . . . In
proportion as he simplifies his life, the laws of the universe will
appear less complex, and solitude will not be solitude, nor
poverty poverty, nor weakness weakness. If you have built
castles in the air, your work need not be lost; that is where they
should be. Now put the foundations under them.

HENRY DAVID THOREAU, WALDEN (1854)

.   .   .   .   .

Sleep not, dream not; this bright day
Will not, cannot last for aye;
Bliss like thine is bought by years
Dark with torment and with tears.

CHARLOTTE BRONTË, *SLEEP NOT* [1846], ST. 1

.   .   .   .   .

Deep, unspeakable suffering may well be called a baptism, a
regeneration, the initiation into a new state.

GEORGE ELIOT, *ADAM BEDE* [1859], CH. 42

.   .   .   .   .

Come, my friends.
'T is not too late to seek a newer world.
Push off, and sitting well in order smite
The sounding furrows; for my purpose holds
To sail beyond the sunset, and the baths
Of all the western stars, until I die.

ALFRED LORD TENNYSON, "ULYSSES," FROM *POEMS OF TENNYSON* (1958), L. 56

.   .   .   .   .

Nature never repeats herself, and the possibilities of one
human soul will never be found in another.

ELIZABETH CADY STANTON, "THE SOLITUDE OF SELF," *THE WOMEN'S COLUMN*
(1892)

.   .   .   .   .

I desire so to conduct the affairs of this Administration that if
at the end, when I come to lay down the reins of power, I have
lost every other friend on earth, I shall at least have one friend
left, and that friend shall be down inside me.

ABRAHAM LINCOLN, *REPLY TO THE MISSOURI COMMITTEE OF SEVENTY* (1864)

. . . . .

From too much love of living,
From hope and fear set free,
We thank with brief thanksgiving
Whatever gods may be
That no life lives forever;
That dead men rise up never;
That even the weariest river
Winds somewhere safe to sea.

ALGERNON CHARLES SWINBURNE, *THE GARDEN OF PROSERPINE* (1866), ST. 11

. . . . .

Providence has hidden a charm in difficult undertakings, which is appreciated only by those who dare to grapple with them.

ANNE-SOPHIE SWETCHINE, IN COUNT DE FALLOUX, ED., *THE WRITINGS OF MADAME SWETCHINE* (1869)

. . . . .

We have a hunger of the mind which asks for knowledge of all around us, and the more we gain, the more is our desire; the more we see, the more are we capable of seeing.

MARIA MITCHELL (1878), IN PHEBE MITCHELL KENDALL, ED., *MARIA MITCHELL* (1896)

. . . . .

Physical suffering apart, not a single sorrow exists that can touch us except through our thoughts.

MAURICE MAETERLINCK, *WISDOM AND DESTINY* (1898)

. . . . .

We work in the dark
we do what we can
we give what we have.
Our doubt is our passion, and
our passion is our task.
The rest is the madness of art.

HENRY JAMES, *THE MIDDLE YEARS* (1893)

. . . . .

The beginning of things, of a world especially,
is necessarily vague, tangled, chaotic,
and exceedingly disturbing.

KATE CHOPIN, *THE AWAKENING* (1899)

. . . . .

When a man or a woman loves to brood over a sorrow and
takes care to keep it green in their memory, you may be sure it
is no longer a pain to them.

JEROME K. JEROME, *ON BEING IN THE BLUES* (1899)

. . . . .

Oh, write of me, not "Died in bitter pains,"
But "Emigrated to another star!"

HELEN HUNT JACKSON, "EMIGRAVIT" (1876), IN EDMUND CLARENCE
STEDMAN, ED., *AN AMERICAN ANTHOLOGY (1787-1900).*

. . . . .

Hold on; hold fast; hold out.
Patience is genius.

COMTE DE BUFFON

. . . . .

It isn't the great big pleasures that count the most; it's making a
great deal out of the little ones.

JEAN WEBSTER, *DADDY-LONG-LEGS* (1912)

. . . . .

My illusion is more real to me than reality.
And so do we often build our world on an error,
and cry out that the universe is falling to pieces,
if any one but lift a finger to replace the error by truth.

MARY ANTIN, *THE PROMISED LAND* (1912)

. . . . .

I found more joy in sorrow
Than you could find in joy.

SARA TEASDALE, "THE ANSWER," *RIVERS TO THE SEA* (1915)

. . . . .

There is in this world in which everything wears out, everyone
perishes, one thing that crumbles into dust, that destroys itself
still more completely, leaving behind still fewer traces of itself
than Beauty: namely Grief.

MARCEL PROUST, *REMEMBRANCE OF THINGS PAST: THE SWEET CHEAT GONE*
(1920)

. . . . .

An idea isn't responsible for the people who believe in it.

DON MARQUIS, *THE SUN DIAL* (1920)

. . . . .

The self is every person's true enemy.

DING LING, "MISS SOPHIA'S DIARY" (1927), FROM *I MYSELF AM A WOMAN*
(1989)

. . . . .

There is far too much talk of love and grief benumbing the
faculties, turning the hair gray, and destroying man's interest in
his work. Grief has made many a man look younger.

WILLIAM MCFEE, *HARBOURS OF MEMORY* (1921)

. . . . .

A belief which does not spring from a conviction in the
emotions is no belief at all.

EVELYN SCOTT, *ESCAPADE* (1923)

. . . . .

When one door of happiness closes, another opens; but often
we look so long at the closed door that we do not see the one
which has been opened for us.

HELEN KELLER, *WE BEREAVED* (1929)

. . . . .

And she saw now that the strong impulses which had once
wrecked her happiness were the forces that enabled her to
rebuild her life out of the ruins.

Ellen Glasgow, *Barren Ground* (1925)

. . . . .

Only when you drink from the river of silence
shall you indeed sing.
And when you have reached the mountain top,
then you shall begin to climb.
And when the earth shall claim your limbs,
then shall you truly dance.

Kahlil Gibran, *The Prophet* (1974)

. . . . .

I hope you have not been leading a double life, pretending to be
wicked and really being good all the time. That would be
hypocrisy.

Oscar Wilde, *The Importance of Being Earnest* (1930)

. . . . .

I postpone death by living, by suffering, by error,
by risking, by giving, by losing.

Anais Nin, *The Diary of Anais Nin, vol. I (1931-1934)*

. . . . .

It's a long old road, but I know I'm gonna find the end.

Bessie Smith, "Long Old Road" (1931), in Chris Albertson, *Bessie* (1972)

. . . . .

Few pleasures there are indeed without an aftertouch of pain,
but that is the preservation which keeps them sweet.

Helen Keller, *Helen Keller's Journal* (1938)

. . . . .

I am one of those who never knows the direction of my
journey until I have almost arrived.

ANNA LOUISE STRONG, *I CHANGE WORLDS* (1935)

. . . . .

Sorrow is one of the vibrations that prove the fact of living.

ANTOINE DE SAINT-EXUPÉRY, *WIND SAND & STARS* (1939)

. . . . .

It is only the happy who are hard, Giles.
I think perhaps it is better for the world if—if one has a
broken heart.
One is quick to recognize it, elsewhere.
And one has time to think about other people,
if there is nothing left to hope for any more.

HELEN WADDELL, *PETER ABELARD* (1933)

. . . . .

No problem can be solved from the same consciousness that
created it. We must learn to see the world anew.

ALBERT EINSTEIN

. . . . .

Failure must be but a challenge to others.

AMELIA EARHART, *LAST FLIGHT* (1937)

. . . . .

The time is approaching when we shall consider it abhorrent
to our civilization to allow a human being to die in prolonged
agony which we should mercifully end in any other creature.

CHARLOTTE PERKINS GILMAN, *THE LIVING OF CHARLOTTE PERKINS GILMAN* (1935)

. . . . .

The heart may think it knows better: the senses know that
absence blots people out. We have really no absent friends.

ELIZABETH BOWEN, *THE DEATH OF THE HEART* (1938)

. . . . .

Death? Why this fuss about death. Use your imagination, try to visualize a world without death!

CHARLOTTE PERKINS GILMAN, *THE LIVING OF CHARLOTTE PERKINS GILMAN* (1935)

. . . . .

The excursion is the same when you go looking for your sorrow as when you go looking for your joy.

EUDORA WELTY, *THE WIDE NET* (1943)

. . . . .

It is far harder to kill a phantom than a reality.

VIRGINIA WOOLF, *THE DEATH OF THE MOTH* (1942)

. . . . .

Freedom of will is the ability to do gladly that which I must do.

CARL JUNG

. . . . .

One is not rich by what one owns, but more by what one is able to do without with dignity.

IMMANUEL KANT

. . . . .

The curious paradox is that when I accept myself just as I am, then I can change.

CARL ROGERS

. . . . .

You must do the thing you think you cannot do.

ELEANOR ROOSEVELT, *YOU LEARN BY LIVING* (1960)

. . . . .

It may be that true happiness lies in the conviction that one has irremediably lost happiness. Then we can begin to move through life without hope or fear, capable of finally enjoying all the small pleasures, which are the most lasting.

MARIA-LUISA BOMBAL, *THE TREE* (1963)

. . . . .

If one changes internally, one should not continue to live with the same objects. They reflect one's mind and psyche of yesterday. I throw away what has no dynamic, human use. I keep nothing to remind me of the passage of time, deterioration, loss, shriveling.

Anaïs Nin

. . . . .

It is good to have an end to journey towards; but it is the journey that matters in the end.

Ursula K. Le Guin, *The Left Hand of Darkness* (1964)

. . . . .

A man must die; that is, he must free himself from a thousand petty attachments and identifications . . . He is attached to everything in his life, attached to his imagination, attached to his stupidity, attached even to his sufferings, possibly to his sufferings more than to anything else . . . . Attachments to things, identifications with things, keep alive a thousand useless "I's" in a man. These "I's" must die in order that big I may be born. But how can they be made to die? They do not want to die. It is at this point that the possibility of awakening comes to the rescue. To awaken means to realize one's nothingness.

G. I. Gurdjieff

. . . . .

If facts are the seeds that later produce knowledge and wisdom, then the emotions and the impressions of the senses are the fertile soil in which the seeds must grow . . . . Once the emotions have been aroused—a sense of the beautiful, the excitement of the new and the unknown,
a feeling of sympathy, pity, admiration or love—then we wish for knowledge about the object of our emotional response.

Rachel Carson, *The Sense of Wonder* (1965)

. . . . .

A man needs a little madness or else he never dares to cut the rope and be free.

NIKOS KAZANTZAKIS, *ZORBA THE GREEK* (1965)

. . . . .

That's what learning is. You suddenly understand something you've understood all your life, but in a new way.

DORIS LESSING, *THE FOUR-GATED CITY* (1969)

. . . . .

Words are less needful to sorrow than to joy.

HELEN HUNT JACKSON, *RAMONA* (1884)

. . . . .

You have to be your own teacher and your own disciple. You have to question everything that man has accepted as valuable, as necessary.

J. KRISHNAMURTI

. . . . .

To laugh is to risk appearing the fool.
To weep is to risk appearing sentimental.
To reach out for another is to risk exposing our true self.
To place our ideas—our dreams—before the crowd is to risk loss.
To love is to risk not being loved in return.
To hope is to risk despair.
To try is to risk failure.
To live is to risk dying.

ANONYMOUS

. . . . .

In space things touch,
In time they part.

ANONYMOUS

· · · · ·

You have to be your own teacher and your own disciple. You have to question everything that man has accepted as valuable, as necessary.

J. KRISHNAMURTI, *FREEDOM FROM THE KNOWN* (1969)

· · · · ·

Never think you've seen the last of anything.

EUDORA WELTY, *THE OPTIMIST'S DAUGHTER* (1968)

· · · · ·

Be joyful because it is humanly possible.

WENDELL BERRY, *A CONTINUOUS HARMONY* (1972)

· · · · ·

A man without ambition is dead.
A man with ambition but no love is dead.
A man with ambition and love for his blessings here on earth
     is ever so alive.
Having been alive,
     it won't be hard in the end to lie down and rest.

PEARL BAILEY, *TALKING TO MYSELF* (1971)

· · · · ·

You need only claim the events of your life to make yourself yours. When you truly possess all you have been and done, which may take some time, you are fierce with reality.

FLORIDA SCOTT-MAXWELL, *THE MEASURE OF MY DAYS* (1968)

· · · · ·

Though friendship is not quick to burn,
It is explosive stuff.

MAY SARTON, *FRIENDSHIPS: THE STORMS, A GRAIN OF MUSTARD SEED* (1971)

· · · · ·

Love doesn't just sit there, like a stone, it has to be made, like bread; re-made all the time, made new.

URSULA K. LAGUIN, *THE LATHE OF HEAVEN* (1971)

. . . . .

What sort of lover am I to think so much about my own
affliction and so much less about hers? Even the insane call,
"Come back," is all for my own sake. I never even raised the
question whether such a return, were it possible, would be
good for her. I want her back as an ingredient in the restoration
of my past. Could I have wished her anything worse? Having
got once through death, to come back and then, at some later
date, have all her dying to do over again? They call Stephen the
first martyr. Hadn't Lazarus the rawer deal?

C. S. LEWIS, *A Grief Observed* (1976)

. . . . .

You will never be happy if you continue to search for what
happiness consists of. You will never live if you are looking for
the meaning of life.

ALBERT CAMUS

. . . . .

But the astonishing or unfortunate thing is that these
deprivations bring us the cure at the same time that they give
rise to pain. Once we have accepted the fact of loss, we
understand that the loved one obstructed a whole corner of the
possible, pure now as a sky washed by rain. Freedom emerges
from weariness. To be happy is to stop. Free, we seek anew,
enriched by pain. And the perpetual impulse forward always
falls back again to gather new strength.

The fall is brutal, but we set out again.

ALBERT CAMUS, *Youthful Writings* (1976)

. . . . .

Some of my best friends are illusions.
Been sustaining me for years.

SHEILA BALLANTYNE, *Norma Jean the Termite Queen* (1975)

. . . . .

Before we were born, we had no feeling: we were one with the universe. This is called "mind-only," or "essence of mind," or "big mind."

After we are separated by birth from this oneness, as the water falling from the waterfall is separated by the wind and rocks, then we have feeling.

You have difficulty because you have feeling.

You attach to the feeling you have without knowing just how this kind of feeling is created. When you do not realize you are one with the river, or one with the universe, you can have fear. Whether it is separated into drops or not, water is water.

Our life and death are the same thing. When we realize the fact we have no fear of death anymore, and we have no actual difficulty in our life.

SHUNRYU SUZUKI, ZEN MIND, BEGINNER'S MIND (1975)

. . . . .

These people realized that when a world goes to pieces and inhumanity reigns supreme, man cannot go on living his private life as he was wont to do, and would like to do; he cannot, as the loving head of a family, keep the family living together peacefully, undisturbed by the surrounding world, nor even can he continue to take pride in his profession of possessions, when either will deprive him of humanity, if not also of his life. In such times, one must radically re-evaluate all of what one has done, believed in, and stood for in order to know how to act.

BRUNO BETTLEHEIM, THE IGNORED LESSON OF ANNE FRANK

. . . . .

I learned to make my mind large, as the universe is large, so
that there is room for paradoxes.

MAXINE HONG KINGSTON, THE WOMAN WARRIOR (1976)

. . . . .

He who celebrates is not powerless.
He becomes a creator because he is a lover.

THOMAS MERTON, LOVE AND LIVING (1979)

. . . . .

The sharing of joy, whether physical, emotional, psychic or
intellectual, forms a bridge between the sharers which can be
the basis for understanding much of what is not shared
between them, and lessens the threat of their difference.

AUDRE LORDE, USES OF THE EROTIC (1978)

. . . . .

Every arrival foretells a leave-taking: every birth a death. Yet
each death and departure comes to us as a surprise, a sorrow
never anticipated. Life is a long series of farewells; only the
circumstances should surprise us.

JESSAMYN WEST, THE LIFE I REALLY LIVED (1979)

. . . . .

A beautiful death is for people who have lived like animals to
die like angels.

MOTHER TERESA, IN KATHRYN SPINKS, FOR THE BROTHERHOOD OF MAN UNDER
THE FATHERHOOD OF GOD (1980)

. . . . .

We can do no great things only small things with great love.

MOTHER TERESA, IN KATHRYN SPINK, ED., IN THE SILENCE OF THE HEART (1983)

. . . . .

Some of what we label psychological or physical disease might more creatively be examined as stalled or overly rapid penetrations of higher energies. Perhaps all of human experience is an interaction between matter and consciousness, and these energies are mediating that.

RICHARD MOSS, *THE I THAT IS WE* (1981)

. . . . .

But the guilt of outliving those you love is justly to be borne, she thought. Outliving is something we do to them. The fantasies of dying could be no stranger than the fantasies of living. Surviving is perhaps the strangest fantasy of them all.

EUDORA WELTY, *THE OPTIMIST'S DAUGHTER* (1968)

. . . . .

The timing of death, like the ending of a story, gives a changed meaning to what preceded it.

MARY CATHERINE BATESON, *WITH A DAUGHTER'S EYE* (1984)

. . . . .

The sheer rebelliousness in giving ourselves permission to fail frees a childlike awareness and clarity . . . . When we give ourselves permission to fail, we at the same time give ourselves permission to excel.

ELOISE RISTAD, *A SOPRANO ON HER HEAD* (1982)

. . . . .

If we forgive God for his crime against us, which is to have made us finite creatures, He will forgive our crime against him, which is that we are finite creatures.

SIMONE WEIL, *FIRST AND LAST NOTEBOOKS* (1970)

. . . . .

In danger there is great power.

AGNES WHISTLING ELK, IN LYNN V. ANDREWS, *CRYSTAL WOMAN* (1987)

. . . . .

Whenever there is chaos, it creates wonderful thinking. I consider chaos a gift.

SEPTIMA POINSETTE CLARK, IN BRIAN LANKER, *I DREAM A WORLD* (1989)

. . . . .

The goal is to live a full, productive life even with all that ambiguity. No matter what happens, whether the cancer never flares up again or whether you die, the important thing is that the days that you have had you will have lived.

GILDA RADNER, *IT'S ALWAYS SOMETHING* (1989)

. . . . .

The life of sensation is the life of greed; it requires more and more. The life of the spirit requires less and less; time is ample and its passage sweet.

ANNIE DILLARD, *THE WRITING LIFE* (1989)

. . . . .

The world of science lives fairly comfortably with paradox. We know that light is a wave, and also that light is a particle. The discoveries made in the infinitely small world of particle physics indicate randomness and chance, and I do not find it any more difficult to live with the paradox of a universe of randomness and chance and a universe of pattern and purpose than I do with light as a wave and light as a particle. Living with contradiction is nothing new to the human being.

MADELEINE L'ENGLE, *TWO-PART INVENTION* (1988)

. . . . .

Wonder and despair are two sides of a spinning coin. When you open yourself to one, you open yourself to the other. You discover a capacity for joy that wasn't in you before. Wonder is the promise of restoration: as deeply as you dive, so may you rise.

CHRISTINA BALDWIN, *Life's Companion* (1990)

. . . . .

Without belittling the courage with which men have died, we
should not forget those acts of courage with which men . . .
have lived. The courage of life is often a less dramatic spectacle
than the courage of the final moment; but it is no less a
magnificent mixture of triumph and tragedy. A man does what
he must—in spite of personal consequences, in spite of
obstacles and dangers and pressures—and that is the basis of
all human morality . . .

In whatever arena of life one may meet the challenge of
courage, whatever may be the sacrifices he faces if he follows
his conscience—the loss of his friends, his fortune, his
contentment, even the esteem of his fellow men—each man
must decide for himself the course he will follow.

The stories of past courage can define that ingredient—they
can teach, they can offer hope, they can provide inspiration.
But they cannot supply courage itself. For this each man must
look into his own soul.

> JOHN F. KENNEDY, *PROFILES IN COURAGE* (1956)

. . . . .

I know for sure
that at the end,
the playful stranger who appears
is not death
but love.

> KATHLEEN NORRIS, "THREE SMALL SONGS FOR THE MUSE," IN MARILYN
> SEWELL, ED., *CRIES OF THE SPIRIT* (1991)

Transformation

. . . . .

. . . for dust thou art,
and unto dust thou shalt return.

GENESIS 3:19

. . . . .

This is the noble truth of sorrow.
Birth is sorrow, age is sorrow, disease is sorrow, death is sorrow
. . . .
in short, all the five components of individuality [khandas] are
sorrow.
    And this is the noble truth of the arising of sorrow.
It arises from craving, which leads to rebirth,
 which brings delight and passion . . . .
    And this is the noble truth of the stopping of sorrow.
 It is the complete stopping of that craving . . . . being
emancipated from it . . . .
    And this is the noble truth of the way
which leads to the stopping of sorrow.
It is the noble eightfold path.

THE PALI CANON (THE SACRED SCRIPTURES OF THERAVADA BUDDHISTS),
SUTTAPITAKA, SAMYUTTA-NIKAYA, 5:421

. . . . .

For certain is death for the born
And certain is birth for the dead;
Therefore over the inevitable
Thou shouldst not grieve.

BHAGAVAD GITA (250 B.C.-A.D. 250), CHAPTER 2, VERSE 27

. . . . .

For when is death not within ourselves? . . . Living and dead are
the same, and so are awake and asleep, young and old.

HERACLITUS (C. 540-C. 480 B.C.), ON THE UNIVERSE, FRAGMENT 78

. . . . .

This embodied [soul] is eternally unslayable
In the body of everyone, son of Bharata;
Therefore all beings
Thou shouldst not mourn.

BHAGAVAD GITA (250 B.C.-A.D. 250), CHAPTER 2, VERSE 30

. . . . .

One word
Frees us of all the weight and pain of life:
That word is love.

SOPHOCLES, OEDIPUS AT COLONUS (406 B.C.), L. 1616,

. . . . .

Friends have all things in common.

PLATO (C. 428-C. 348 B.C.), DIALOGUES, PHAEDRUS, SEC. 279

. . . . .

You cannot conceive the many without the one.

PLATO (C. 428-C. 348 B.C.), DIALOGUES, PARMENIDES 166

. . . . .

No man is wise enough by himself.

TITUS MACCIUS PLAUTUS (254-184 B.C.), MILES GLORIOSUS, ACT III, SC. III

. . . . .

Not lost, but gone before.

LUCIUS ANNAEUS SENECA (8 B.C.-A.D. 65), EPISTLES 63, 16

. . . . .

Every time an earth mother smiles over the birth of a child, a
spirit mother weeps over the loss of a child.

ASHANTI SAYING

. . . . .

Behold, I shew you a mystery;
We shall not all sleep, but we shall all be changed,
In a moment, in the twinkling of an eye, at the last trump:
for the trumpet shall sound,
and the dead shall be raised incorruptible, and we shall be
changed.
For this corruptible must put on incorruption,
and this mortal must put on immortality.
So when this corruptible shall have put on incorruption,
and this mortal shall have put on immortality,
then shall be brought to pass the saying that is written,
Death is swallowed up in victory.
O death, where is thy sting?
O grave, where is thy victory?

I CORINTHIANS 15:51-55

. . . . .

What is life? A madness.
What is life? An illusion, a shadow, a story.
And the greatest good is little enough:
for all life is a dream,
and dreams themselves are only dreams.

PEDRO CALDERÓN DE LA BARCA (1600-1681), *LIFE IS A DREAM*, ACT II, L. 1195

. . . . .

There is great skill in knowing how to conceal one's skill.

FRANÇOIS, DUC DE LA ROCHEFOUCAULD, *REFLECTIONS; OR, SENTENCES AND
MORAL MAXIMS* (1678), MAXIM 245

. . . . .

We know the truth, not only by the reason, but by the heart.

BLAISE PASCAL, *PENSÉES* (1670), NO. 282

. . . . .

No man is an island, entire of itself; every man is a piece of the continent, a part of the main; if a clod be washed away by the sea, Europe is the less, as well as if a promontory were, as well as if a manor of thy friends or of thine own were; any man's death diminishes me, because I am involved in mankind; and therefore never send to know for whom the bell tolls; it tolls for thee.

JOHN DONNE, *DEVOTIONS* (1623). XVII

. . . . .

He who binds to himself a joy
Does the winged life destroy;
But he who kisses the joy as it flies
Lives in eternity's sunrise.

WILLIAM BLAKE, *POEMS* (WRITTEN C. 1791-1792) FROM BLAKE'S NOTEBOOK.
SEVERAL QUESTIONS ANSWERED, NO. 1, HE WHO BINDS

. . . . .

Man was made for joy and woe,
And when this we rightly know
Through the world we safely go.

WILLIAM BLAKE, "AUGURIES OF INNOCENCE," L. 56, *POEMS FROM THE PICKERING MANUSCRIPT* (C. 1805)

. . . . .

The voice of Nature loudly cries,
And many a message from the skies,
That something in us never dies.

ROBERT BURNS, "NEW YEAR'S DAY" (1791), ST. 3

. . . . .

To see a world in a grain of sand
And a heaven in a wild flower,
Hold infinity in the palm of your hand
And eternity in an hour.

WILLIAM BLAKE (1757-1827), POEMS FROM THE MSS. *AUGURIES OF INNOCENCE*, L. 1

. . . . .

I accept the universe!

MARGARET FULLER, IN PERRY MILLER, ED., MARGARET FULLER (1963). TO
THOMAS CARLYLE (1846)

. . . . .

It is eternity now.
I am in the midst of it.
It is about me in the sunshine;
I am in it, as the butterfly in the light-laden air.
Nothing has to come; it is now.
Now is eternity;
Now is the immortal life.

RICHARD JEFFERIES, THE STORY OF MY HEART (1883)

. . . . .

Genius . . . means little more than the faculty of perceiving in
an unhabitual way.

WILLIAM JAMES, THE PRINCIPLES OF PSYCHOLOGY (1890)

. . . . .

Grief can take care of itself, but to get the full value of a joy
you must have somebody to divide it with.

MARK TWAIN, FOLLOWING THE EQUATOR (1897). CAPTION FOR AUTHOR'S
PHOTOGRAPH ON SHIPBOARD, FRONTISPIECE OF FIRST EDITION. VOL. II,
PUDD'NHEAD WILSON'S NEW CALENDAR, CH. 12

. . . . .

The mind of man is capable of anything because everything is
in it, all the past as well as all the future.

JOSEPH CONRAD, HEART OF DARKNESS (1902)

. . . . .

The whole drift of my education goes to persuade me that the
world of our present consciousness is only one out of many
worlds of consciousness that exist.

WILLIAM JAMES, THE VARIETIES OF RELIGIOUS EXPERIENCE (1906)

. . . . .

Many times in the history of human thought a belief once heretical has become a universally accepted truth . . . . The history of science is partly the history of paradoxes becoming commonplace and heresies becoming orthodoxy.

ANONYMOUS

. . . . .

That is happiness; to be dissolved into something complete and great.

WILLA CATHER, *My Antonia* (1918)

. . . . .

This is the true joy in life, the being used for a purpose recognized by yourself as a mighty one; the being thoroughly worn out before you are thrown on the scrap heap; the being a force of nature instead of a feverish selfish little clod of ailments and grievances complaining that the world will not devote itself to making you happy.

GEORGE BERNARD SHAW, *Man and Superman* (1903), EPISTLE DEDICATORY

. . . . .

What we have once enjoyed we can never lose.
All that we love deeply becomes a part of us.

HELEN KELLER, *We Bereaved* (1929)

. . . . .

To mention a loved object, a person, or a place to someone else is to invest that object with reality.

ANNE MORROW LINDBERGH, *North to the Orient* (1935)

. . . . .

Music is our myth of the inner life . . . .

SUZANNE K. LANGER, *Philosophy in a New Key* (1942)

. . . . .

Has the body a soul? No. The soul has a body. And well does that soul know when this body has served its purpose, and well does that soul do to lay it aside in high austerity, taking it off like a stained garment.

LUCIEN PRICE, *LITANY FOR ALL SOULS* (1945)

. . . . .

Stars and blossoming fruit trees:
Utter permanence and extreme fragility give an equal sense of eternity.

SIMONE WEIL, *GRAVITY AND GRACE* (1947)

. . . . .

We shall not cease from exploration
And the end of all our exploring
Will be to arrive where we started
And know the place for the first time.

T. S. ELIOT, "LITTLE GIDDING," *FOUR QUARTETS.* (1942)

. . . . .

It is immediately apparent . . . that this sense-world, this seemingly real external universe, though it may be useful and valid in other respects, cannot be the external world, but only the self's projected picture of it . . . . The evidence of the senses cannot be accepted as evidence of the nature of ultimate reality.

EVELYN UNDERHILL, *MYSTICISM* (1955)

. . . . .

Discovery consists of seeing what everybody has seen and thinking what nobody has thought.

ALBERT SZENT-GYORGYI VON NAGYRAPOLT, IN I. J. GOOD, ED., *THE SCIENTIST SPECULATES* (1962)

. . . . .

Love always opens up the intellect and gives it the freedom of genius.

ERNEST DIMNET, *ART OF THINKING* (1961)

. . . . .

I am convinced that the universe is under the control of a loving purpose, and that in the struggle for righteousness man has cosmic comradeship. Behind the harsh appearance of the world, there is a benign power.

MARTIN LUTHER KING, JR., *STRENGTH TO LOVE* (1963)

. . . . .

The conservative impulse will make us seek to deny the loss. But when this fails, it will also lead us to repair the thread, tying past, present and future together with rewoven strands of meaning.

PETER MARRIS, *LOSS AND CHANGE* (1974)

. . . . .

It is not only by the questions we have answered that progress may be measured, but also by those we are still asking. The passionate controversies of one era are viewed as sterile preoccupations by another, for knowledge alters what we seek as well as what we find.

FREDA ADLER, *SISTERS IN CRIME* (1975)

. . . . .

I cannot exist without in some sense taking part in you, in the child I once was, in the breeze stirring the down on my arm, in the child starving far away, in the flashing round of the spiral nebula.

CATHERINE KELLER, *FROM A BROKEN WEB* (1986)

The lonely experience gives a person back to himself, affirms his identity, and enables him to take a step toward a new life. The experience of love is the spark and energy of excitement and joy, it is what makes friendship a lifetime value and what makes activity purposeful. A balance is essential. Exaggeration of either loneliness or love leads to self-denial and despair. Love has no meaning without loneliness; loneliness becomes real only as a response to love.

CLARK MOUSTAKAS, *LONELINESS AND LOVE* (1986)

Suffering and anguish, while being lived, can be almost unbearable; but in time, through a mysterious process of awareness and transcendence, the hurt moves forward into the bliss of liberation and into a new zest for living. Then there is a passionate claim to human existence that brings with it a feeling of relationship. The self that does not reach out to encounter and include others is, indeed, still mourning, still split and suffering. To come back to the human community, one must know the clear visions of loneliness and solitude and the joy of being born again. One must also know the depths of loving unconditionally and of being unconditionally loved, of forming new bonds with others.

CLARK MOUSTAKAS, *LONELINESS AND LOVE* (1986)

May all sentient beings be well
and enjoy the root of happiness:
free from suffering and the root of suffering.
May they not be separated from the joy beyond sorrow.
May they dwell in spacious equanimity
free from craving, fear and ignorance.

BODHISATTVA VOWS (ADAPTED)

. . . . .

The difference between transformation by accident and transformation by a system is like the difference between lightning and a lamp. Both give illumination, but one is dangerous and unreliable, while the other is relatively safe, directed, available.

MARILYN FERGUSON, *THE AQUARIAN CONSPIRACY* (1980)

. . . . .

I would like to believe when I die that I have given myself away like a tree that sows seeds every spring and never counts the loss, because it is not loss, it is adding to future life. It is the tree's way of being. Strongly rooted perhaps, but spilling out its treasure on the wind.

MAY SARTON, *RECOVERING* (1980)

. . . . .

Perhaps you feel you are the only one in the universe but out of your loss is an interconnectedness with all humanity—for you are ONE with everyone who has ever mourned.

RUSTY BERKUS, *TO HEAL AGAIN* (1989)

. . . . .

I still miss those I have loved who are no longer with me but I find I am grateful for having loved them. The gratitude has finally conquered the loss.

RITA MAE BROWN, *STARTING FROM SCRATCH* (1988)

. . . . .

Apparent failure may hold in its rough shell the germs of a success that will blossom in time, and bear fruit throughout eternity.

FRANCES ELLEN WATKINS HARPER (1875), IN FRANCES SMITH FOSTER, ED., *A BRIGHTER COMING DAY* (1990)

· · · · ·

Spiritual energy brings compassion into the real world.
With compassion, we see benevolently our own human
condition and the condition of our fellow beings. We drop
prejudice. We withhold judgement.

CHRISTINA BALDWIN, "LIFE'S COMPANION," *JOURNAL WRITING AS A SPIRITUAL QUEST* (1990)

· · · · ·

Grace happens when we act with others on behalf of our world.

JOANNA MACY, *WORLD AS LOVER, WORLD AS SELF* (1991)

· · · · ·

Do not stand at my grave and weep;
I am not there, I do not sleep.
I am a thousand winds that blow.
I am the diamond glints on snow.
I am the sunlight on ripened grain.
I am the gentle autumn's rain.
When you awaken in the morning hush,
I am the swift uplifting rush
Of quiet birds in circled flight.
I am the soft stars that shine at night.
Do not stand at my grave and cry;
I am not there. I did not die.

ANONYMOUS